HIDD

Bu

at St. Ann's, Cape Breton Island

From *Hidden Heritage:*

"Standing here, in this place at this moment, it is impossible not to be deeply moved. Yet it is not the beauty of time or place, the piper's tune nor the pathos of romantic fancy which strikes so deeply to the very centre of our being.

"It is its associations, rather than the place itself, which stab to the heart. For I am a Canadian, and all about me is the story of my country."

View of Port Dauphin (St. Ann's Harbour), 1713

HIDDEN HERITAGE

Buried Romance *at* St. Ann's, Cape Breton Island

JAMES B. LAMB

WITH AN APPENDIX OF CONTEMPORARY VOICES
AND "A WALKING TOUR"

PHOTOGRAPHS, DRAWINGS, AND MAPS

Breton Books

Editor: Ronald Caplan

Production Assistance: Bonnie Thompson

Cover Photograph: Warren Gordon

Cover Drawing: Jean-Luc Chassé

Our thanks to Jean-Luc Chassé for sharing his extraordinary work, vision, and drawings of early European history at St. Ann's Bay. He is a founding member of the Englishtown Historical Society.

For guidance on this project, thanks to Joan MacInnes, museum curator, and Norman MacInnes, maintenance supervisor, at the Gaelic College of Celtic Arts and Crafts; to W. James MacDonald and Katherine Robinson, both of the Englishtown Historical Society; and to Sam and Sandy MacPhee at the Gaelic College. Thanks as well to the staff at Fortress Louisbourg National Historic Park for help in locating information; and to Nimbus Publishing for permission to offer this new expanded edition.

The Canada Council for the Arts | Le Conseil des Arts du Canada

We acknowledge the support of the Canada Council for the Arts for our publishing program.

Tourism and Culture

We also acknowledge support from Cultural Affairs, Nova Scotia Department of Tourism and Culture.

Canadian Cataloguing in Publication Data

Lamb, James B., 1919-2000

Hidden heritage

1st ed.

Originally published: Windsor, N.S. : Lancelot Press, 1975.
ISBN 1-895415-52-7

1. St. Ann's Bay Region (N.S.) — History. 2. Englishtown (N.S.) — History.
I. Title.

FC2345.S227L35 2000 971.6'93 C00-950106-1
F1039.S18L35 2000

CONTENTS

NOTE: This is an updated and corrected edition of *Hidden Heritage*, with considerable new material. Author James B. Lamb uses the word "today." While some of the trails and ruins of foundations can be expected to be quite overgrown, much of what he talks about can be found. And his invitation to walk and remember and dream is rich, and worth the challenge.

◆ 1 ◆

The Fort in the Forest

Fort Sainte-Anne ◆ 1629-1641

MOST PEOPLE COME UPON IT for the first time from Highway 105, the easternmost part of the Trans-Canada Highway, as it sweeps, in steep-sloping curves, around the seaward side of Kelly's Mountain between Baddeck and Sydney. The most conscientious driver, preoccupied with the steep grades of this superb stretch of road, cannot help but become aware of the spectacular nature of the scenery at his elbow, through occasional glimpses of the void below; few can resist pulling into the well-marked roadside parking area which has become one of the most popular "look-offs" on the east coast.

Whatever the time of day, the nature of the weather, the season of the year, this is one of the most magnificent views the country can offer. On a moonlit night, its black-on-silver beauty is breathtaking; on a sunny summer day it unrolls a panorama of blues and greens that recedes to the farthest horizon. Three hundred years ago a French nobleman declared it the most beautiful harbour in all the world, and its beauty still gladdens the eye and lifts the hearts of hundreds of thousands of passersby.

Yet few of the multitudes who see it every year have any conception of the significance of this beautiful place in the history of Canada and, indeed, of North America. If you stand at the road's edge above the whole vast prospect, you look out to your right over a shimmering sea rimming a view of headlands, mountainous and magnificent, reaching away in endless series to melt into the blue of the distant horizon. In front a broad, deep bay, backed by wooded hills, is crossed by a bar of sand and shingle; a long, slim sandspit, pierced by only a single narrow channel, it encloses a great natural harbour which stretches away, sheltered by high hills and fed by a broad rivermouth on the far shore, for miles to the left. A ferry boat plies back and forth across the narrow channel, offering a short cut connection with the Cabot Trail, Cape Breton's famed scenic route, but otherwise there is little to break the idyllic stillness of the scene, and nothing at all to indicate the part this lovely place has played in the struggle for the New World.

Yet once this quiet bay was the bastion of French power in America; French fleets moored here, years before Louisbourg was built; near where the ferry now docks, a French fortress once stood. A century before that, British prisoners-of-war built a fort here to serve their French captors, and here began the great Jesuit mission to Christianize the natives that carried two Frenchmen from this lovely place to the horrors of death in the fires of the Iroquois on far-away Georgian Bay. Here occurred the first European murder recorded in the New World, and a subsequent mystery that still puzzles men's minds. Here, on the hillside below, a true-life giant lived and died, and over there, on that wooded peninsula jutting into the harbour, a religious fanatic set up a community of Highlanders a century after the French had left, and terrorized them with the fear of God. On that shelving beach, these doughty people built a ship with their own hands and sailed off to newly-discovered New Zealand, a world away, and on that jutting point opposite, their descendants built the great wooden ships that made Canada a maritime power in the days of sail. To this sheltered bay came the first German colonists, the last of the Indian fishing settlements, and the terrible scourge of professional hunters who, in the late eighteenth century, exterminated the moose in a few bloody years for the sake of a gourmet's fancy.

Of all these centuries of history, the tourist sees only a few names on a map. For this is the Bay of St. Ann's, on the eastern shore of Cape Breton Island, and nowhere else in Canada is there so rich a hidden treasure of colourful history to reward the interested visitor, nor such a wealth of ruins and remains, unexcavated and unexplored. They are more than the ruins of mere buildings, however; they are the wrecks of empires and crusades, of men's dreams and hopes, for always through the centuries the bay has been a gateway which, for all its promise, led nowhere. St. Ann's is history's beautiful deceiver.

Half a mile to the west of the look-off is the turn for Englishtown, the tiny community which stands today amid the ruins of the past. The road runs along a high bluff that rims the waters of the landlocked bay; a bay so beautiful it is hard to remember that it was for centuries a notable haven, and for six years was the cornerstone upon which was based the New World strategy of the greatest military power in Europe. On the outskirts of Englishtown, St. Mark's Church stands on a rocky promontory between the road and the water, occupying one of the oldest Indian sites in the area. Here, according to the first French explorers, a community of Indians was located when the European ships arrived; a community which apparently depended more upon the sea for its sustenance than the land. To this day, the well near the Church is known as "Indian Well." The whole shoreline of St. Ann's has been lived on intermittently by Indian bands over the centuries, apparently, but the Church point appears to have been settled more or less continuously for a very long period of time. Two hundred years after the French first noted the Indians living on the promontory, Indians were still encamped there, still living principally on fish and shellfish long after their contemporaries had reverted to primitive crop-raising and hunting for existence. White men came and white men went, but the Indian fishermen went on more or less forever. Today, however, only the Church occupies a site which has been intensively inhabited for unknown centuries.

Englishtown today is principally a ferry terminal, surrounded by a scattering of houses. At the roadside immediately to the west of the shore, a cairn and bronze plaque have been erected by the Government of Canada [1930] which briefly outlines the history of the early French fort and subsequent development. It is in this area that the earliest European settlement was located, and it is here that the general nature of the French plan can best be seen.

Behind the cairn, a rocky hillock crowns a small point jutting out into the harbour, and in the grass on every side can still be seen the rectangular mounds and depressions which mark the outlines of the little settlement which grew up inside the first fort. The hillock itself, the single highest point of the generally low-lying foreshore and situated directly opposite the sandspit which all but encloses the harbour, is the key to the French position. Here stood the main battery commanding the narrow harbour entrance, with eight cannon behind embrasures, and a log stockade extending back towards the line of the modern road to make a rectangle, within which were located a barracks, a chapel, a magazine, a bakery and other auxiliary buildings, and it is fascinating to stroll about the site and attempt to discern the layout of the place from the scattered mounds and pits which are all that are left today.

Here, on the 28th of August, 1629, arrived an armed French ship, crammed with men and deep laden with supplies, commanded by a most remarkable leader. Captain Charles Daniel of Dieppe was a man of intelligence, ability and decision, and was to display these qualities time and again during his service in the New World. He had been sent out from France in command of a two-ship expedition loaded with men and supplies for Champlain's new base at Quebec, but it seems likely that his instructions also included some reference to the need to support the French fishery, as well as the supply route from France through the Gulf of St. Lawrence, by establishing a strongpoint at the easterly extremity of Nova Scotia. In any event, Daniel's ships left Le Cap de Baye in France on June 26, 1629, but became separated in the thick and frequent fogs on the Grand Banks a few weeks later. Fog was followed by wind; in a series of heavy gales Daniel's unwieldy and deep-laden ship was driven south from his intended course, sighting the coast of Cape Breton on the morning of the first clear day following the long period of bad weather.

Coming abeam of St. Ann's, he noted the apparent haven offered by sheltering cliffs and sandspit, and brought his battered ship in to anchor and refit.

Next morning, in his usual decisive manner, he sent an armed body of ten men ashore to scout southward along the coast to make contact with Indians and learn what he could of the general situation, concerning both Champlain's forces at Quebec and the dangerous British settlements further south in New England. While this scouting body was away, he put in hand the work of watering ship and refitting his stormbattered vessel, and became deeply impressed with the security and amenity of his snug anchorage, which, he learned, was called Sipo by the Indians (pronounced Seeboo), and later spelled "Ciboux" by French cartographers.

In a few days his scouting party returned with disturbing news. James Stuart, the Scottish Lord Ochiltree, had just completed a fort at Baleine, a small inlet just to the north of present-day Louisbourg, and the presence there of his armed garrison of Scot settlers posed a threat both to the French fishery and to the supply line to Quebec. Daniel now displayed his customary initiative and decision; removal of this threat obviously was a more urgent matter than the delivery of his shipload of supplies to the Quebec garrison, and he acted accordingly. On the shores of St. Ann's he drilled and equipped his men for their new role, while his scouts kept watch on the British position. When he learned that the last British ship had left the bay at Baleine, Daniel moved swiftly, and on September 8, 1629, he anchored just out of gunshot from the British fort. A landing party of sixty men, backed up by the ship's guns, quickly overcame the resistance of the little garrison and seized and destroyed their new fort. Adding its supplies and men to his own, Daniel sailed back to his base at St. Ann's, determined to fortify it and make it strong enough to deter any further attempts by the British to menace the supply line and fisheries of New France. [For original descriptions, see "Appendix."]

Here, where only a few mounds disturb the smooth surface of the ground today, Daniel built his fort to command the finest anchorage on the eastern seaboard. Daniel put fifty of his own men and twenty of his Scottish prisoners to work on the fort, using mostly soldiers and other landsmen, while his sailors were busy landing supplies and readying the ship for the winter crossing to France.

It was more than a mere trading fort which Daniel set out to found here; he intended to establish, as his orders no doubt stated, a secure and defensible anchorage which could serve in peace as a safe haven for French fishing vessels and a staging point for supply ships bound westward to Quebec and eastward to France, and in time of war as a base for a French fleet. The easternmost shore of Cape Breton was an ideal site for the purpose, since it commanded the principal entrance to the Gulf of St. Lawrence and intervened between this and the growing British power to the south. Daniel seems to have been intrigued by the possibilities of Spanish Bay, the future site of Sydney, but to have decided that its wide entrance was much too difficult to defend with the limited armaments at his disposal. By contrast, St. Ann's was ideal, its single narrow entrance easily commanded by a simple battery at its mouth.

His practiced eye quickly picked out the little rocky knoll, even today still called "The Lookout," as the key to the position, dominating both the lower land to the rear and the narrow harbour entrance in front, and it was here that he set up his main strength, a battery of eight cannon. It is interesting to note that local residents still refer to a low part of the shoreline here as "Number One gun," and still salvage from the sea occasional iron cannonballs, relics of the old French battery.

Using his British prisoners as an unwilling but available work force, Daniel cleared the little apron of land behind the knoll, where the white house and its lawns now lie, and set up a simple fort, log stockades to landward and earthen ramparts facing the sea. Inside he built barrack accommodation to house a minimum of fifty men; a chapel for the Jesuit missions which he was instructed to found there; a safe, strongly-built magazine for the considerable supply of gunpowder necessary both for the fort's guns and garrison as well as that needed to replenish the supply of visiting men o'war; and the bakery, cookhouses, latrines and auxiliary buildings needed for a permanent garrison.

In a matter of weeks, the work was finished; anxious to return to France before the winter gales made the crossing hazardous, Daniel sailed away, leaving behind him a secure and well-located French base garrisoned by forty soldiers, commanded by Captain Gaude, a professional military officer; two priests of the newly-invigorated Jesuit order, Father Bartholomew Vimont and Father de Vieuxpont, who were to organize the stupendous task the order had set itself, the Christianizing of the New World's heathen hordes; and all the supplies and munitions brought from France for the purpose—the whole establishment under the command of an adventurous aristocrat, Sieur Claude de Beauvas.

Before leaving, Captain Daniel named his new base and dedicated the little chapel, the first of what was hoped to be a network of thousands in New France, after St. Ann, at the request of Louis's mother, Queen Ann of Austria. One of the rectangular mounds which can still be seen faintly in the grass west of the present building may well mark the site of this simple but significant church, built here at the wishes of the royal mother of one of the most powerful monarchs who ever lived.

Standing today on the little waterfront knoll, and looking toward the modern roadway, it is not difficult to picture the situation of the little fort which stood here nearly three hundred and fifty years ago. The southern limits of the stockade could not have been much beyond the present roadway, and the line of the seaward limit is plain to see. Most of the area is open today, unencumbered by modern buildings, and it would be difficult to find a more appealing and rewarding site for unimpeded excavation. Until the site is dug, however, one can only speculate as to which bump or depression might be all that remains of which of the known structures put up here in that first settlement.

On the evidence of his record, Beauvas does not seem to have been a particularly able or enterprising commandant. Left in command of a well-founded fort, amply provisioned and well-defended, and with every resource of a well-watered, wooded and sheltered area at his back and a harbour teeming with fish and a foreshore famous for its shell fish at his front, his little post seemed far more securely launched than most of these new European ventures into the raw American wilderness. In particular, he had the benefit of the support and experience of an established community of friendly Indians in the immediate neighbourhood. Yet despite this, the initial winter was a crippling one for the garrison; scurvy, that bane of settlers and sailors deprived of the greens and root crops available the year-round in their European homelands, enfeebled the whole community, and before spring many died of it. Yet local Indians knew the cure, and others before Beauvas had found through experiment that the American wilderness provided a variety of effective remedies; only sailors cut off from shore and living on salt rations needed to die of scurvy in the seventeenth century. Whatever the circumstances, Beauvas's little force suffered severely throughout the long Nova Scotian winter, in a climate much milder and less rigorous than that endured by contemporary French settlers inland to the north and west.

Yet an even more tragic occurrence can be laid at the door of the Sieur de Beauvas. For serious quarrels broke out in the confined community, a sure indication of poor morale, and morale must ever be the prime concern of any commander of a remote station. Worse, the tragedy concerned not merely the soldiers who comprised the disciplined backbone of the community, but their officers. At some time during the second winter, when the recall of Fathers Vimont and Vieuxpont had left the fort without a priest, Captain Gaude, commander of the military detachment and an infantry officer of considerable experience, shot and killed his second-in-command, Lieutenant Martell. It was the first murder of a European by a European recorded in the New World.

The circumstances of the killing were never set down, or at least if they were, they did not survive to the present day. Given the military traditions of the time and the peculiar circumstances of the station, it is possible that Martell was shot in a duel with his commanding officer, although against this must be set the obvious and instant odium which the killing seems to have incurred. For Gaude was instantly deprived of his position and was imprisoned to await trial in the spring, when French ships were expected to return with officers aboard of sufficient rank and seniority to try him. However it occurred, this slaying was a momentous, if sinister happening in the history of the New World; somewhere under the grass surrounding this little knoll today lie the bones of a French infantry officer, victim of the first white murder in Canada. In such a limited area, they may well be found someday if the site is ever excavated, along with the remains of his fellow-soldiers who died in that first cruel winter of garrison duty.

Spring brought release, at last, from the confinements and sickness of the long winter. It also brought Captain Daniel, back from France with a complement of priests and settlers to establish here the religious and commercial base of what was hoped to become a thriving bastion of a trading empire, and the centre of the Jesuit Christianizing effort.

On each of his spring arrivals in those first two years at the little colony, Daniel must have been dismayed to find the shaken condition of the garrison, which he had left each time comfortably established a few months before. On his first return in the spring of 1630, he found many of his soldiers dead of scurvy, and many more still not fit for duty, having been enfeebled by the disease. On his second return, he learned of the acting Commander's killing of his second-in-command; furious, he ordered him instantly to be placed under close arrest, which infers that previously Gaude had simply been confined to barracks. We do not know what passed between Daniel and Beauvas, the inept commandant of the colony, but Daniel can hardly have been impressed by his conduct of matters.

Now occurred something which has intrigued

historians ever since. For Captain Gaude, who most by now have been under no illusions about his ultimate fate, somehow managed to escape from his prison before he was brought to trial, and disappeared from the fort and from history. Perhaps someone friendly to him connived at his escape; it is unlikely that he could have managed the thing by himself. But where did he go? What could he do? There was not another European within hundreds of miles, and without arms and provisions he could not hope to have sustained himself in the wilderness for long.

No clue remains to us; Gaude, the first Canadian murderer, becomes also the first Canadian murder mystery. Yet surely there was only one thing he could have done; he must have made his way to the nearby Indian settlement and managed to secure help in keeping out of sight; perhaps he was taken by Indians there to some other native community further inland. In all likelihood he became the first white man to "go native," perhaps marrying an Indian woman and begetting the first of the children of mixed blood who were ultimately to replace the pure-blooded Indian stock throughout the Maritimes. Somewhere Gaude must have found an obscure native grave, far from his home in France and indeed from all European civilization; his only memorial a strain of genes in the Indian bloodstock.

In the long run, it can be said that, although he escaped execution, Gaude paid with his life for this crime; indeed, it may well have been that the swift extinction of the bullet might have been the more merciful.

Daniel wasted little time in looking for the

missing prisoner. His men were soon busy clearing the forest outside the stockade walls and erecting timber buildings to house the settlers whom he had brought with him, and who were settled on small clearings all about the fort, which was henceforth to be only the military centre of the new colony. The cleared ground, at first so small, was to increase with each passing year, and traces of these first farms, and of the foundations of the little buildings located on them, are still to be found in the vicinity today. Racks were set up on the beach for drying fish, the only way then available for preserving them for the long run back across the Atlantic, and sometime during this summer the first of the French fishing vessels were based here for the seasonal fishing in the Gulf and the nearby Grand Banks. Trade was also begun with the Indians, and the bales of furs gathered at the little fort made up the first cargo to be shipped back to France from St. Ann's Bay.

But the most significant changes at Fort Sainte-Anne involved the religious community. A series of seven Jesuit priests arrived to minister to the settlers and Indians at St. Ann's during the first few years, the little chapel having become the centre of a full-fledged mission. Living quarters were set up outside the fort walls, where presumably there were fewer restrictions on space. Long and arduous expeditions by canoe were begun to carry the word of God to Indian communities along the Bras d'Or Lakes and further inland, but details of the mission activities are not known. One of the new Jesuits was Antoine Daniel, brother of the expedition's leader, and already one of the most promising and zealous of the missionaries. He seems to have shared his brother's energy and purpose, and he was destined to push his way ever westward, in the very forefront of his order's Christianizing crusade, until he reached Fort Sainte-Marie, "St. Marie Among the Hurons," on the shores of Georgian Bay, the westernmost point of all New France. Here, with his brother priests Brébeuf and Lalemant, as brave and dedicated as he, he met a martyr's death at the hands of the dreaded Iroquois. Standing in the sunlit serenity of St. Ann's today, it seems an incredibly long way, in space and time, back to the melting marshland of St. Marie, St. Ignace and St. Joseph far away on the inland sea, and to the thin smoke rising from those dreadful stakes on a grey March morning more than three hundred years ago. Yet that great mission, undertaken at such cost and doomed to sustain such crushing failures, received its first great impetus here at this very place, its details worked out within the walls of one of those little rectangular mounds which now scarcely ripple the surface of the Englishtown grass. [St. Anthony Daniel was killed July 4, 1648, aged 47; he was beatified by Pius XI in 1925 and canonized in 1930.]

Champlain arrived at Fort Sainte-Anne in June 1633; when he left, he took with him two priests to work among the Indians at Quebec and in Huronia, Champlain's new venture. Each summer saw the same pattern of growth and activity, which was to continue for the next dozen years. Sometime during this period there was another notable arrival; Simon Denys, a member of one of the most adventurous and enterprising families in the history of New France, settled here and quickly established himself as the most capable and successful farmer in the colony. Not only did he clear land for cultivation, but he also planted and sustained the first orchard—a plantation of apple trees which was to become famous over the years. A brother, Nicolas Denys, came to the new colony as a captain in an infantry regiment, and in this capacity he surveyed the whole harbour and surrounding coastal area of St. Ann's—the first really thorough survey made. An enthusiastic promoter of the possibilities of the site, he was later created Sieur de Fronsac and made governor of Isle Royale by the King of France. Trade with the Indians flourished; the shore became covered with the drying racks used by increasing numbers of fishermen who made St. Ann's their base during the long summer fishing season.

But in 1641 there came a change. The Jesuits found their mission, at the uttermost extremity of a vast continent, an awkward base from which to reach natives other than those on Cape Breton Island itself. The little mission was closed, and its priests scattered to posts further inland. Even more significant, French military policy changed; new bases on the shores of southern Newfoundland were both closer to France and to the trade routes of their rivals, the British now firmly entrenched along the southern and eastern shores of Newfoundland. A great concentration of power was built up by the French at a strong base at Placentia, and it was to there that the garrison of St. Ann's was eventually transferred. The little settlement on the tip of Isle Royale, as Cape Breton Island was called, dwindled to a handful of farmer-fishermen, augmented by the crews of visiting fishing vessels in the summer season. The log stockade of the fort itself fell into decay, and the empty mission dissolved in ruin, yet the indomitable Simon Denys continued to fish and farm here for another twenty years. The apples from his orchard were by now famous throughout the fishing fleets, and were much sought after by fruit-starved fishermen and seamen weary of months on salt rations. For a space of half a century, while British and French strove for mastery of the New World's burgeoning trade, St. Ann's was left in peace, its wooded loveliness broken only by a handful of tiny farms scattered about the sagging walls of its empty fort and abandoned mission.

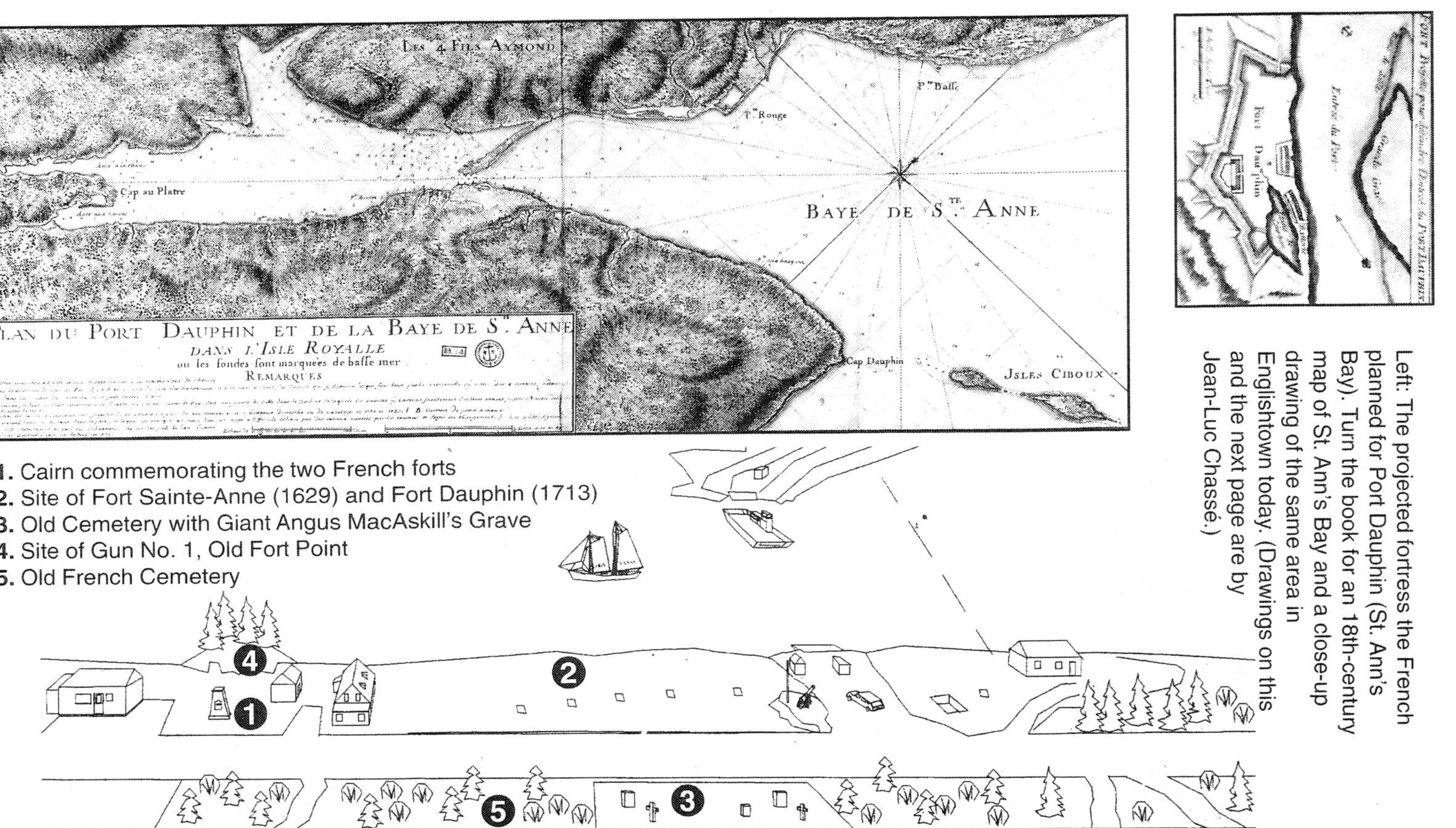

1. Cairn commemorating the two French forts
2. Site of Fort Sainte-Anne (1629) and Fort Dauphin (1713)
3. Old Cemetery with Giant Angus MacAskill's Grave
4. Site of Gun No. 1, Old Fort Point
5. Old French Cemetery

Left: The projected fortress the French planned for Port Dauphin (St. Ann's Bay). Turn the book for an 18th-century map of St. Ann's Bay and a close-up drawing of the same area in Englishtown today. (Drawings on this and the next page are by Jean-Luc Chassé.)

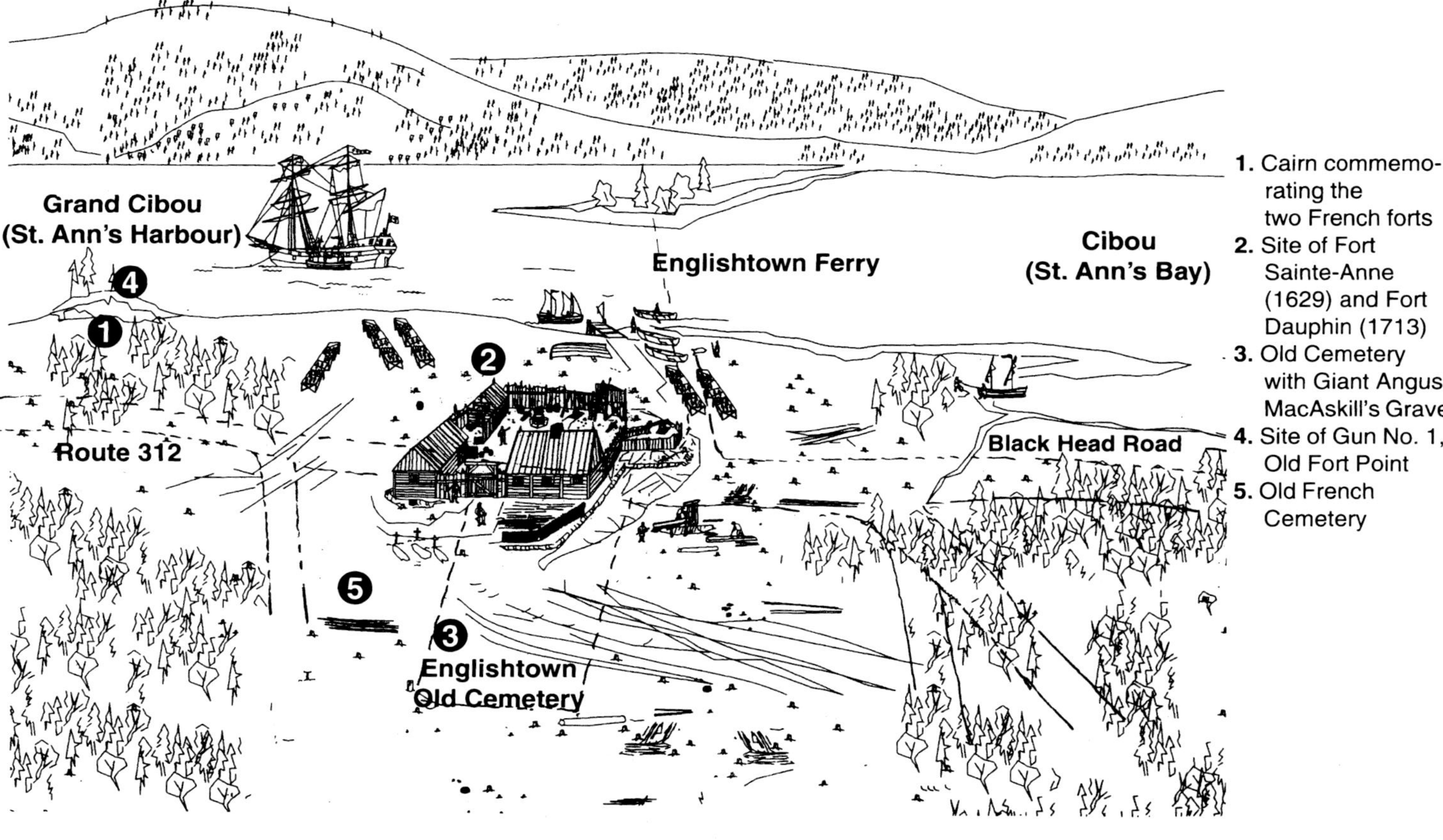
Grand Cibou
(St. Ann's Harbour)
Englishtown Ferry
Cibou
(St. Ann's Bay)
Route 312
Black Head Road
Englishtown
Old Cemetery
1. Cairn commemorating the two French forts
2. Site of Fort Sainte-Anne (1629) and Fort Dauphin (1713)
3. Old Cemetery with Giant Angus MacAskill's Grave
4. Site of Gun No. 1, Old Fort Point
5. Old French Cemetery

Rev. Norman McLeod; "The Red House" overlooking Black Cove; stone wall around graves of John Robertson and his wives; monument at site of "The Big Church."

Original building at the Gaelic College of Celtic Arts. See an aerial view of the Gaelic College today, on the Back Cover of this book.

Angie and A. W. R. MacKenzie, founders of the Gaelic College. Painting by Mary Stanbury Bethune.

Nova Scotia Premier Angus L. Macdonald unveils the monument to Rev. Norman McLeod and his followers, at the Gaelic College in 1939.

Angus MacAskill, the Cape Breton Giant; the MacAskill homestead; and the Giant MacAskill Museum at Englishtown.

The Cairn at Englishtown located at The Lookout—the central bastion of the defences of Fort Dauphin.

Fr. Pacifique (with the white beard) dedicates the Historic Sites and Monuments Board cairn at Englishtown, 1930. Below: the old sailing wharf, circa 1975, South Haven (South Gut). The shed and wharf extension are now gone.

The grave of Angus MacAskill, the Cape Breton Giant, overlooks the ferry at Englishtown and the site of the French forts.

◆ 2 ◆

The Bastion of New France

Fort Dauphin ◆ 1713-1778

IN 1713 BEGAN the momentous series of events which was to convert St. Ann's from a forgotten colonial backwater into a centre of world-wide significance, the keystone of the entire French empire in the New World. The flowering was to be brief, but nonetheless impressive.

France had lost her struggle against the British in Newfoundland; by the Treaty of Utrecht she was stripped of her territories there and on the American coastline, and confined to Isle Royale itself; the rugged little island of Cape Breton had small attraction for the British, now busy with the developing trade of New England. Somewhere on the coast of this wooded, mountainous island the French must establish a base if they were to provide effective naval support for their citadel at Quebec, and the network of trading posts and frontier forts it sustained in central Canada. Given the effective cannon ranges of the time, there were only two possibilities open to the French planners for good anchorages capable of easy defense: Louisbourg, the fog-plagued, inaccessible harbour at the southeast corner of Isle Royale, or St. Ann's Bay, where the ruins of their first fort still existed.

Almost without exception, the planners opted for St. Ann's. Governor Nicolas Denys reported that St. Ann's was so much better a site than Louisbourg that "an expenditure of ten thousand here can achieve more than the spending of a million can effect at Louisbourg." From Quebec, Governor Vaudreuil wrote endorsing this view, and recommending, in the strongest terms, that Fort Sainte-Anne be made the base which would secure Quebec's seaward communications.

Nor were the experts, sent by the French authorities to survey the situation, any less enthusiastic about the possibilities of the St. Ann's site. Joseph Guyon, a pilot sent from Quebec, reported that the depth of 14 to 15 fathoms at the harbour entrance was ample for any ship ever built, while the anchorage inside was sheltered and clear of shoals and obstructions. The foreshore provided space for up to fifty ships to dry their catch of fish on drying frames, he noted carefully. A civil engineer from France, M. L'Hermite, claimed that St. Ann's was one of the finest harbours in all America, offering, in addition to its natural anchorage and defenses, wood, water, cleared farmland, apples—those apples again!—plaster and coal. The ruins of the old fort could easily be made defensible again, he added, and could be incorporated into a modern system of defense. The mention of plaster among the amenities of the place is interesting, for the whole of the area of St. Ann's and the Bras d'Or is notable for its outcroppings of gypsum, now extensively exploited by modern industry.

The most favourable report, however, was probably that of a French army officer, Denys de la Ronde; none other than the grandson of old Simon Denys who had settled here some eighty years before. De la Ronde found, to his huge delight, that the trees planted by his grandfather so long ago were still bearing apples, and recorded in his diary that he had picked them himself and found them delicious.

"It is the most beautiful harbour in all the world," reported this much-traveled officer.

Today in the area of modern Englishtown, there are plenty of old apple trees. Is it possible that some of them might still carry on the strain first introduced here, centuries before, by Simon Denys? Certainly, as we shall see, trees of the old stock were still here in the middle of the nineteenth century.

In Paris, the enthusiastic reports on the advantages of St. Ann's produced the inevitable decision; the fort at St. Ann's, to be renamed Fort Dauphin in honor of the King's son, rather than the more difficult Louisbourg, was to be made the bastion of France's power on the Atlantic shore of the New World.

It is curious to a modern viewer of the scene how so many qualified authorities could have overlooked the fatal flaw in St. Ann's as a naval base. For facing the opposite shore as one stands at the Lookout today, on the site of the old French fort, one can see the entrance of the North River away to one's left. Even the most casual survey must have shown this to be a river of considerable size, deep, and fast-flowing, and consequently that the water of the bay must be largely fresh and thus very vulnerable to frost in winter. Given the landlocked nature of the site, and the high ground to the westward which prevents an offshore wind from clearing any ice from the harbour, and the narrow entrance to the eastward which makes it correspondingly easy for an onshore wind to keep ice penned up as in a corked bottle, it is strange indeed that so many engineers and seamen of experience should not have sensed the base's Achilles heel. For, as they should have perceived, St. Ann's is peculiarly susceptible to severe icing; its landlocked and sheltered location retains the ice throughout most winters. As a naval base, St. Ann's is a dead loss for three to four months in the year.

But in faraway Paris, none of this could have been understood, and the authorities on the spot do not seem to have included such cautionings in their reports. In 1713 the French government cleared its garrisons from around Placentia in Newfoundland, and sent them, together with cannon, ships and munitions, to establish the new base of Fort Dauphin. From this point onward, the fort left its outpost status, and entered on a new era as a major fortress and bastion of empire. The era was destined to be short, but it was undeniably distinctive; never, before or since, were so many people concentrated in one place on the shores of this lovely bay. For six brief years Fort Dauphin became a place of consequence to the capitals of Europe.

As the backbone of the base, a fortress incorporating the latest theories of Vauban—the French fortification genius who revolutionized the concept of military defense—was to be constructed. Two distinct and different plans were drawn up and survive to this day in the archives of Ottawa, and there are conflicting theories as to which projected plan was eventually adopted. However, an investigation of the site today leaves little doubt that the smaller and simpler of the designs was the one chosen, a verdict which is substantiated by a chart of the area drawn up much later, in 1778, by which time the fortress would have long been a ruin. This chart, accurate in all its ascertainable essentials, although to a small scale, shows a fort rectilinear in outline, with wedge-shaped bastions, and in walking over the ground today this seems to be borne out by the nature of the visible ruins.

The plan for this fort, drawn up on Order 299 of the Depot des Fortifications des Colonies by J. Juteau and dated 1715, shows a strong earthwork battery on the Lookout site, where the earliest French fort still stood. It is square in plan, with thick earthen ramparts ramped outward to deflect cannonshot, and it forms the core or citadel of the whole position, its guns commanding the narrow harbour entrance, and its triangular bastions and curtain wall making it defensible independent of the remainder of the fort. The outer rampart runs east and west from this strong point along the rim of high land above the foreshore, terminating in a corner bastion to the west above a small creek which forms a natural line of defence, and ending in a similar bastion to the east where the land slopes away to a large brackish lagoon, lying between the sea and the high land. From these bastions a rampart runs at roughly right angles to similar bastions some hundreds of feet to the south, where a rampart parallel to the seaward wall encloses the fort's central court, defended along its length by two projecting triangular bastions.

The whole forms a simple yet strong defensive work, its whole function being to close the harbour mouth to hostile ships by the concentrated fire of its central battery, while affording sufficient landward strength to resist any attack by landing parties from ships lying off out of cannon range. An interesting refinement suggested on the alternative plan calls for two blockhouses on the sandspit opposite the fort, to prevent any landing thereon. It is not known whether, in fact, these interesting embellishments were ever constructed, and the low sand and shingle beach today provides no clues, without excavation. A large magazine, for storing the considerable quantities of powder needed for such a base, was built in the northeast angle of the walls in the shelter of a large corner bastion, with a bakery and a forge in the same general area. The rather unusual grouping—gunpowder and fires make uneasy bedfellows, surely!—seems to have been adopted in order to shelter all these vulnerable and essential services in the lee of what high ground existed on the spot.

On the whole, the fortress as drawn, and presumably as built, impresses as straightforward and strong, taking full advantage of the ground to command the harbour entrance with maximum firepower, and of the natural defences provided by the deep ravine and streambed to the west and the lagoon and its low ground to the east. Its long south wall, without any such natural advantages, is given maximum protection by two rampart bastions and two diamond-shaped corner bastions, projecting so as to give enfilading fire along the whole length of the rampart. Presumably the ramparts were of earth, dug from a ditch which became, with its glacis or bank opposite, a part of the defences, and revetted either in wood or stone. The magazine, presumably, would have been dug into the earth and roofed over with corbelled stone, while the other buildings would have been of timber, perhaps on fieldstone foundations like so many buildings in the area right down to the present day.

A weakness of the position, although one that would only become of consequence in the event of a siege by land forces, is that it is commanded by the rising ground to the southward, where a range of low hills rises up to a steep wooded ridge. Musketry from this elevated position would sweep the whole of the southern rampart, and cannon of any size here could completely dominate the entire fortress. The shortcoming in defences was provided against on one of the plans drawn, by the addition of outworks—either detached ravelins or blockhouses—atop a couple of the higher hillocks south of the curtain wall.

A similar flaw, permitting an enemy to occupy ground commanding the defences, was to prove the Achilles heel of Louisbourg, not once but twice, but here at Fort Dauphin the issue was never put to the test. Yet at both sites one can detect the folly of preparing plans in Paris, for sites far away in the New World, on the basis of faulty and incomplete reports; such a centralized bureaucracy must of necessity lack the "feel" of a site, and hence be unable to adapt itself completely to the lay of the land. For all its sophisticated complexity, Louisbourg was a house of cards; any schoolboy viewing the site could quickly see its glaring vulnerability to an attacker approaching overland.

Here at Fort Dauphin, steps may well have been taken to defend the high land to the south; there is a local tradition, even today, that the remains of defence works can still be found on some of the wooded hills in the rear.

While work on the defences went on, involving large numbers of men, both civilians and soldiers alike, a great many other projects were put in hand. A shipyard was laid out just to the westward of the new fortress. Here a variety of small craft were built for servicing the community, in addition to a magnificent flush-decked frigate of thirty-six guns, the largest and finest French warship yet undertaken in the New World. Her construction is clear evidence of the degree of organization prevailing at the site, for the building, fitting out and arming of such a big ship entails a great deal of skilled labour as well as the availability of a large and varied stock of supplies. Only a major base could have undertaken the building and completion of such a powerful fighting vessel.

Hand-in-hand with this military and naval activity went a large-scale program of settlement, to provide the agricultural basis necessary to sustain the fortress and dockyard. Some score of farms were hacked out of the bush in the area about the growing fortress, many of them, no doubt, occupying the overgrown sites of former farms dating back to the earliest days of the French settlement nearly a hundred years before. But the most successful of all was the tremendous feudal farm cleared and organized by the Chevalier de Boularderie on the nearby island that still bears his name. This enormous estate eventually entailed more than 100,000 acres of rolling arable land, farmed by tenants as well as by twenty-five personal retainers, who in addition operated wind and water mills, a large dovecote, a dairy, and extensive kitchen gardens. The chevalier himself occupied a gracious house set on the hillside overlooking the lovely waters of the Great Bras d'Or for more than thirty years, and the wheat he developed and grew on his magnificent farm became famous on two continents. More than sixty years later, long after the last Frenchman had left the place, a British surveyor reported that the grain, by then growing wild in the fields, was the finest wheat in America.

Today Boularderie Island presents one of the most settled and cultivated appearances of any part of Cape Breton, and the patterns of the old French fields can still be clearly seen. The superb masonry foundations of the large spring house, which provided not only clear water but cool storage for perishables, can be seen today close to the modern roadway, along with the mounded foundations of the great manor house itself.

For six years, beginning with the landing of the Placentia garrisons here in 1713, Fort Dauphin flourished as the Atlantic base of New France, the chief ornament of Isle Royale and principal North American staging point for the ships and troops of Europe's greatest military power. Yet from the beginning its fatal shortcoming must have been evident to all: from December through to late April the harbour was locked in the grip of thick ice. British fleets could pass unchallenged through the Gulf of St. Lawrence while French ships were icebound in St. Ann's, and supply ships from France had to stand off until late into spring, waiting for the ice to clear.

The end came in 1719 with a decision made in Paris; the principal French power was to be shifted to a new base to be built at Louisbourg, plagued by fog and poor land communications but relatively ice-free the year around. In a matter of months, Fort Dauphin, the focus of such intense activity for the past six years, reverted to the status of a colonial backwater; a settlement of farmer-fishermen hacking a living from small farms clustered around an abandoned fortress; a base where seasonal French fishermen could dry their fish, mend their gear—and enjoy a good apple. Henceforward, the fortunes of Fort Dauphin, like that of the French empire itself in the New World, began a steady decline. With the sack of Louisbourg [1745] by an amateur army of New England farmboys and apprentices, the writing was obviously on the wall; static fortifications, however elaborate, were no match for growing British seapower. Louisbourg's second and final fall [1758], to General Wolfe and his army enroute to bigger things on the Plains of Abraham, snuffed out the last French hopes in Isle Royale, and the crumbling ramparts and sagging barracks of Fort Dauphin were never put to the test of attack.

The British arrived peacefully on the scene in

1760. The great estate of Boularderie was abandoned, its sturdy farmers settling, with others from remote parts of Isle Royale, in communities along the northwest coast of the island, on what is still called "The French Shore." The officers, the noblemen, the military garrisons, all made their way back to their French homeland; only a handful of fishermen-farmers clung to their clearings on the shore of St. Ann's Bay. A British officer, Captain Holland, made a survey of the area in the late '60s, but his report to the British government brought little response in the way of English settlers. A French naval chart of the area, drawn in 1778, shows some twenty buildings, presumably farmhouses, scattered about the ruins of the empty fortress. There is no sign of the naval shipyard, of the lumber mill, the forge or the other facilities constructed here half a century before. As a military and naval base, Fort Dauphin had died.

It is from the chronicles of the Church that we have the best impression of the declining years of Fort Dauphin. Father Dominique de la Marche, a man of culture and refinement, was stationed at the Fort Dauphin mission, which he had helped to rebuild with his own hands, with a chapel only thirty-five feet long, from 1716 until 1730, the period which saw the rise and fall in the fortunes of the French base. He was succeeded by Father Le Breton in 1734, and by Father Moisson in 1753, by which time there were no more than thirty-eight people living there the year around, although there were still large numbers of fishermen based there during the summer.

Its bones still lie about us today, undisturbed

by the excavator's trowel. Centuries of decay, of heaving frosts and driving rain have leveled the buildings, filled the ditches; determined and deliberate destruction by generations of farmers has reduced the earthworks and permitted the plough to restore most of them to the level from which they were originally dug. What man could not do, nature quickly achieved. Generations of trees have sprouted and died in the old ramparts, reducing them to mere mounds; land has been returned to forest, cleared and ploughed, and returned to woodland again in the long march of the years. Today, what was once a strong fortress capable of resisting cannonshot, and its surrounding community, is merely a pattern of mounds and pits and thickets; a network of lines and dimples drawn in the grass by the low rays of the setting sun.

Yet for all of that it is fascinating to stroll over the site, and speculate on the location of the principal features of the defences. Perhaps nowhere else in Canada is there such a rich and varied and virgin site, embodying the varied usage and habitation of centuries, and embracing features that are clerical and secular, naval and military, commercial and agricultural.

Close to today's abandoned ferry wharf at Englishtown lies the entrance of the little creek which is the principal feature of all the old French plans, and which clearly delimits the westernmost wall of Fort Dauphin. Immediately to the east, as one follows the present roadway parallel to the waterfront, a large hummock dominates the shoreline. A great heap of grass-covered rubble, it is undoubtedly the western corner bastion of the fortress, and from it one can follow with one's eye the whole shoreward line of the ramparts, extending eastward. Between this point and the white house near the cairn, situated about half-way along the front of the position, the ground today is covered with grassland, tall and rough on the shore but mown into a smooth lawn all about the neat white building, between the road and the waterfront. The remains of some dozen rectangular buildings are clearly seen under this lawn; some are unquestionably associated with the last and greatest phase of the fortress, but others are probably the remains of even older buildings, erected by Captain Daniel inside his first, smaller fort which also stood on this site, and which must have already been ruins when the last fortress was constructed here in the eighteenth century.

Further along, the so-called Lookout—a rocky outcropping dominating both shore and land—marks the centre of the position, the site both of the main battery of the fortress and of the entire stockaded post first built early in the seventeenth century. Here there is such a wealth of ruin, of pits and mounds and tumbled stone, that it is difficult to distinguish individual features. This part of the place is best seen from the foreshore, or from the deck of a ferry making the crossing of the harbour entrance. The outline of the long earthwork ramp, which was the seaward face of the fortress, can still easily be recognized beneath the evergreen scrub that now mantles it. In the rear of this place, at the roadside, stands the official cairn and plaque that marks the site.

Walking eastward along the road, one comes to

a low, triangular tumulus of tumbled rubble, now covered in deep grass [a cannon is now positioned on the summit]. This is certainly the site of the diamond-shaped corner bastion that marked the eastward limit of the fort, and from its top one can look back towards the modern buildings and trace the mounded remains of the seaward rampart which once joined it to the main battery. Immediately beyond and below the bastion, the ground slopes away [near the place where the present cable ferry docks]—and on this low ground the great brackish lagoon still lies today as it did three and a half centuries ago, protecting the east flank of the fort. In every detail, its outline appears just as it did on the plans of the Parisian cartographers. It is interesting to reflect that this insignificant-appearing little pool should have been a significant factor in the calculations of some of the best military brains of the age, and a tactical feature of prime importance for more than a hundred years.

The southern portions of the fortress are not so immediately apparent, being obscured by rising ground, tall grass and undergrowth, as well as a few modern buildings and two small cemeteries. It is easiest to trace the western rampart, running along the eastern bank of the little creek mentioned earlier. Here the mounded line of the wall can still be followed, and in many places the tumbled stone, presumably of the old revetting, still lies in piles among the thickets that line the bank. Some distance inland, in cropped meadowland, the low mounded bank of a diamond-shaped corner bastion can still be made out; an ancient tree grows on its summit. This is surely the northwest corner of Fort

Dauphin, but the position is further complicated by the remains of a rectangular foundation pit and a considerable accumulation of tumbled stone, presumably once again the remains of the revetting necessary to hold the sharpcut earthwork in place.

The remaining corner bastion is obscured by a cemetery, still in use, but the line of the rampart runs across a series of fields and meadows, where it has been virtually eradicated by generations of ploughing. Yet despite this intensive and long-continued farming, now virtually ended, the whole area abounds in mounds and bumps and depressions, which only an excavation could interpret. These mark the internal arrangements of the eighteenth-century fortress, as well as some of the external buildings that once surrounded the seventeenth-century establishment.

Yet far and away the most intriguing, and puzzling, remains are those that abound in the wooded hills to the south. These are accessible from a variety of modern lanes and roadways, but also by an ancient overgrown roadway, well ramped and graded, leading into the woods from the banks of the creek. On every hand there are the remains of ancient clearings, old stone fences, the outlines of forgotten foundations. Most of these must be the sites of the farms referred to in the old French chronicles, but some may well be the blockhouses shown in one of the 1715 plans for fortification of the site. For it must be borne in mind that only the *projected* plans for the fortress have survived; the final outline of the fortifications as actually constructed are still something of an enigma, the only evidence, beyond that of what remains, being the general outline sketched in 1778, when the fortress was already an abandoned ruin.

There are traces of wide and well-built roadways deep in these wooded hills, which may, of course, belong to a much later era. But most baffling of all is the overgrown remains of a long, straight stone wall, which runs roughly east and west for a considerable distance. Was it intended as a defensive work, crowning the crest of the commanding ridge? It seems most unlikely, unless it was possibly associated with a blockhouse at each end, and yet it seems far too large and long and solid a work to be simply a farm enclosure.

More easily comprehensible are the relics inevitably turned up by ploughing, by domestic digging and by fishing in the area. Cannonballs are a recurring find, right down to the present day; one nearby resident has several of them in a shed, and others are ornaments in homes as far away as Baddeck. Most of these are discovered on the foreshore, uncovered by a scouring tide. Some of them may have come from the warships which were anchored in the bay two and three centuries ago, but many more must surely have found their way there from the long row of cannon which once lined the seaward battery. Sword bayonets, musket barrels, buckles and hobnails are frequent finds and proof of the site's military character, but there have been a multitude of objects, ranging from vast numbers of nails and metal spikes, rusted together, to doorlocks, knives and forks, and metal pans and pots. Such finds were once commonplace, but as farming in the area has declined in recent years, so has the frequency of such discoveries.

Yet all these have been merely chance finds, of the most superficial nature. When you stroll today across the Englishtown pastureland, you walk among the tumbled remains of a puzzle of the most intriguing sort; a puzzle whose solution is half-guessed, but whose final clues are hidden by a paltry few inches of grass and topsoil. One can hardly wait to see this ancient conundrum made clear, as it must be, one day.

St. Ann's Harbour
in Cape Breton Island
from A. F. Church's map
Victoria County, circa 18

◆ 3 ◆

The Restless Shepherd

Reverend Norman McLeod: Assynt to Black Cove ◆ 1780-1827

APPROPRIATELY for this abandoned imperial outpost, Fort Dauphin lies on a dead-end road, which ends near Cape Dauphin a few miles further east. To drive back westward is to return to the present day past all the milestones of the years intervening between the abandonment of the fort in the mid-eighteenth century and today. There is Englishtown itself, named after the half-dozen English families who settled here in 1778, after Wolfe had won Canada for the British. They were joined by an Irish family and, later, by a solitary American from Virginia, the settlement's only bachelor. It was this lone Virginian who featured in the tiny community's first domestic tragedy; he was found dead in his cabin one morning, having hanged himself.

Somewhere along the shores skirted by the modern highway was the camp of a band of professional hunters, ruffians of mixed blood, who single-handedly exterminated all moose in Cape Breton. In the winter of 1789 these vandals killed more than nine thousand moose, leaving the antlers and carcasses intact where they fell, taking only the skin, which sold for ten shillings apiece, and the projecting and prominent upper lip or nose. This was used to make a soup, called Moufle, which was considered a great delicacy in Europe, and which provided these rascals with their principal source of income. After wiping out the island's moose in a few brief winter seasons, these butchers moved on to Newfoundland, where they were to eradicate hundreds of thousands more wild animals.

Along the south shore the road passes Willhausen Point, where the first German settlers, a family of that name, established themselves in 1790, and flourished there for more than half a century. Further along, an enterprising fisherman from the Island of Jersey built a fishing station late in the eighteenth century at the beach which still bears his name: Ramos Beach.

At the upper end of its long southern arm, St. Ann's Bay is divided into two small bays, called today South Gut and North Gut, by a wooded promontory jutting out from the western shore. It is approached by the Cabot Trail, which crosses the South Gut on a modern causeway before climbing a steep grade to the Gaelic College, high on the crest of a wooded hill. Immediately south of the college grounds, an unmarked gravel-surfaced road leaves the highway and runs eastward, through woodland, to a pattern of overgrown hillside fields sloping down to the waters of St. Ann's Bay and the South Gut. From the top of the hill, one looks over the full prospect of St. Ann's Bay, with the site of Fort Dauphin in the middle distance.

More than a hundred and fifty years ago—in September 1819—on a bright, sunny morning, a little eighteen-ton schooner picked its way up the harbour, past the ruins of the French fort on its deserted point, past the scattered cabins of the tiny community at Englishtown, and into the sunlit serenity of the South Gut. She came to anchor just off a sandy beach in the shallow bay enclosed in an elbow of the promontory, which can still be seen from here, and landed her little party of eight, led by a powerfully-built, greying man of dour and commanding presence. They were men from the Highlands of Scotland, part of the new wave of Scottish immigrants who were to transform the empty Canadian wilderness. Their leader, who called himself "Reverend" but was accredited to no established church, was Norman McLeod. One of the most remarkable men who ever lived in Canada, he was to leave an abiding mark in three continents; a mark that exists to this day.

Norman McLeod was born in 1780 in a crofter's hut of stone and sod on the rocky headland of Stoer Point in the parish of Assynt; a bare, poverty-stricken, windswept headland of rock jutting out into the Atlantic waters of the North Minch, in northwest Scotland. The harsh, cruel environment shaped the character of the man; McLeod had all the dour obstinacy and flinty independence of his fellow Highlanders, together with a power of intellect and strength of will that set him apart in a crofting community of illiterate farmers and fishermen. Above all, he possessed a religious fanaticism and moral arrogance which dominated his intensely religious, even superstitious neighbours; his strength, both physical and intellectual, made him a born leader among a people starved for leadership. From the beginning, McLeod felt himself born to lead, and indeed his career is one of the most remarkable testimonials to the dominating power of the intellect; a power which, although expressed only by eye and tongue, could create fear and even terror in the hearts of multitudes, and could move hundreds to give up all they possessed to follow him literally around the world.

To apprehend the otherwise incredible story of this man's achievements on this now-placid piece of land, it is necessary to understand something of the background against which they took place.

In the latter part of the eighteenth century the Highland clan system, a heroic form of society that had survived since the Iron Age in the remote Scottish mountains, had been finally and tragically shattered at Culloden; a badly frightened Hanoverian monarchy was vengefully stamping out its last vestiges, even to the banning of kilts and tartans. The heads of the clans, who had for two thousand years held their position by unwritten traditions of sufferance, were transformed by British law into regional lairds, the Caledonian equivalents of the established nobility south of the border, and the clan lands, held in common for communal use since time immemorial, were given over to them as simply private estates. Thousands of clansmen, deprived at a stroke of their traditional focus of social and economic life, found themselves dispossessed from lands in which they no longer had any right, their crofts cleared away to make room for the flocks of sheep which were the basis of the new wealth in the Highlands. To such men, hungry for land, the limitless acres available for the taking in the New World were an irresistible lure, and beginning with the *Hector*'s voyage to Pictou in 1773, they flocked to Canada's primitive east coast in increasing numbers.

But it was no mere need for land to farm that brought McLeod to the Canadian wilderness. From an early age, he had known that his vocation lay with the exercise of his mind, not his hands, and he had attempted to become, first, a clergyman, and later, a teacher. In each his obvious gifts had made their mark, but in both instances his moral intensity, his fierce intolerance, his disdain of compromise and delicate sense of integrity made him an impossible compatriot for men who, however varied their outlook, had agreed to accept the common discipline of a codified religion or established syllabus.

McLeod was incapable of any relationship other than that of master and faithful slave, with himself ever the master, whose role, divinely assigned, was the chastening of an obedient flock toward some vaguely sensed, and sometimes changing, goal.

He found such a flock, docile and even eager for his leadership, ready to hand. Inured for generations to endure cold and hunger and hardship without complaint, to bear the worst that cruel man and nature could inflict, the native obstinacy of the hardy Highlander bred a curious passivity, an unquestioning acceptance of his lot, however hard, that contrasted sharply with the aggressive urge to better his life that characterized his Lowland contemporary. Centuries of nomadic existence and communal ownership of every sort of property had given the Highland Scots a disdain for the material amenities, the vanities and fripperies by which others seemed to set such store. To such men, name and reputation was all; with genealogies extending back over centuries, they accounted themselves the equal of any man alive, and the superior of most, however blue their blood, and they cared nothing for mere material possession, or what other men reckoned wealth. Defoe writes of seeing, in the eighteenth century streets of downtown Edinburgh, "a man in mountain habit, armed with a broadsword, a target, a pistol; at his girdle a dagger, and staff, walking down the High Street as upright and haughty as if he were a lord, and withal driving a cow." Yet for all this fierce pride and independence, his indifference to material progress and a resultant disinclination to work for anything beyond his minimum physical needs, the Highlander had little ambition beyond the limits of the clan and community. For the high direction of the communal effort, he relied upon leadership from on high. The outside world, and his clan's response to it, was understood to be the concern of his leaders, and lay largely beyond the realm of the individual Highlander's interest.

Such leadership, provided for centuries by the head of the clan who could commit his following to war or peace with a single word, was by now largely taken over by the Highland ministers of the church. These unique preachers of the faith were, by the very nature of their circumstances, remarkable men, enjoying a status not unlike that of the Biblical prophets whose words they gloried in. Morally and intellectually, they dominated their isolated congregations, and had to be prepared to champion their every word against the searching questions of "the men"—those fervent worshippers present in every congregation, set aside from their fellows by their religious fanaticism, who could be relied upon at every service to rise and "speak the Question." Thus every sort of spiritual problem would be debated and wrestled with by minister and questioner, for the enlightenment of the congregation.

Few of the ministers in the Highlands were members of the Scottish established church; it was almost impossible to persuade men of such dissident and uncompromising beliefs to accept a common discipline. More than that, the Scottish church in the lowlands had undergone a humanizing and liberalizing experience late in the eighteenth century; it was this Lowland "softness" which determined Norman McLeod, after six years of preparation, to abandon his intended ministry with the established church. To the Highlander, and especially so intolerant and arrogant a one as McLeod, such humanist concepts were "decadence"; the Highland creed was the hard one of the Old Testament as expounded by John Calvin, worshipping not a "gentle Jesus, meek and mild," but a jealous and vengeful Jehovah, cruel but just. There was nothing of love in the Highland creed; such a softness had no place in the world of rock and cold and misery that they knew. It was a creed of hate and punishment and eternal damnation for backsliders which the Highland dominie preached, and none preached it with such relish as the young teacher-preacher Norman McLeod at Ullapool, near Loch Broom, where his weekly denunciations of his moderate parish superior drew huge congregations of shocked parishioners to his independent chapel, but ended in his expulsion from both pulpit and classroom.

But McLeod was not alone in his adherence to an older, more virulent creed, entirely at odds with modern concepts of Christians worshipping a Prince of Peace. Nothing could better exemplify the hard Highland belief with its intolerance and vengeful jealousy, than the eighteenth-century Scots dominie on a hill overlooking Carrowkeel, where the gallant Montrose, Scotland's greatest soldier, had finally fallen to a treacherous Duke of Argyll suborned by English money. Montrose's army had included large numbers of Irish Catholic soldiers, and after the battle Argyll's men ruthlessly butchered all the women and children in the Irish camp. Surveying the scene, where screaming Papist children were being butchered by knives and axes, the Scots church minister turned to an appalled spectator and, rubbing his palms approvingly, observed: "Ah, the Laird's work gangs bonnily on."

Such were the Christian concepts common to the Highlands at the time of Norman McLeod's brief Scottish ministry.

At thirty-six years of age, married to a sickly wife and with three young children, McLeod found himself in desperate straits. A brilliant teacher and preacher, he had closed both professions to himself by his own intolerance of any authority save his own, and by an inability to compromise remarkable even among a contentious and obstinate people. There was nothing for him in Scotland, so that he took the only course open to him. In July 1817 he set sail in the barque *Frances Ann* for Pictou, the new Scots settlement in Nova Scotia.

It was not a happy choice for a man determined to build and cherish a congregational flock faithful to the old tenets of the Highland church. Pictou was booming, money pouring in from a lumber trade to Britain that made farming or fishing, other than for the merest necessities, a waste of time. Every man in Pictou seemed to spend most of his time lumbering, either away in the winter camps or in the booming yards and sawmills that clustered along the waterfront. Rum was available in plenty from the West Indies, where Pictou ships carried on a year-round trade, but above all, there was the new and infectious freedom of the New World; a tendency to throw off the old restraints, the old inhibitions of the homeland.

Worst of all, from Norman McLeod's point of view, there were already three Scots church ministers established in Pictou, inevitably leading to three dissident Scot congregations. Yet by McLeod's standards, all three could be tarred with the same brush as "humanists"; soon his own new church—for he never hesitated a moment in gathering his flock about him—became celebrated for the torrents of abuse which he poured out on his fellow ministers. This was powerful preaching, in the old Highland style, and quickly his congregation grew, both in numbers and in spellbound devotion.

As it grew, so did its minister's determination to lead it to some more hallowed spot, where he could build about his parishioners a wall of geographical isolation to match the defences his preaching fashioned against moral or spiritual corruption. His wife and family had joined him in Pictou, and in his second year of restless residence in this boisterous, bustling boom town he was also joined by a group of his former parishioners from Assynt. These were men of some substance and learning, most of them boyhood friends of McLeod; the Munro brothers, Alex, Donald and John; Donald MacLeod, known as "The Squire" and a man of proven business capacity; and Norman MacDonald. With these men at his side, Norman McLeod felt ready to strike out for new fields.

Curiously enough, the original objective of the expedition which he organized was Ohio, far away in the American Midwest. It was intended to sail down the eastern seaboard into the Gulf of Mexico to the mouth of the Mississippi, and up that to the Ohio, as far as that river proved to be navigable. Undaunted by the prospect of so great a voyage, the congregation set to work to build a suitable boat: a solid eighteen-ton schooner which was designed to take only the first advance party, the balance to follow once a settlement had been effected. Jeering neighbours, aware of McLeod's prophecies of doom for the benighted people of wicked Pictou, named the little boat "The Ark," as he prepared it against the day of destruction, and the name stuck. It was the *Ark*, therefore, which brought Norman McLeod and his advance party—which included Squire MacLeod as sailing master, Norman MacDonald as navigator, Hugh Matheson as chief officer, Alex MacDonald and John MacLeod, the Squire's son, among others—to the mouth of St.

Ann's Bay, where they anchored for the night after catching a great many cod.

Next morning, the beauty of the place enchanted them. Awestruck, they sailed up six miles of sheltered water, overhung by wooded highlands. The waters were alive with fish, the sunlit beaches backed by silent forests. To the mariners fresh from the raw ugliness of a lumber boomtown, it seemed a veritable heaven on earth; all notions of the long trip to remote Ohio vanished on the spot. The crew came ashore in what is now Black Cove, and after the briefest consultation, decided to stay. This very spot was to be the new home for Norman McLeod's devoted congregation.

Each man, during that long afternoon, paced out a plot of land on the part of the shoreline which he had selected as a home site for his family. Norman McLeod took for himself the peninsula on which the party had landed; its central position was an obvious advantage for the leader, and for the church where the flock would receive their spiritual guidance. On each plot, a clearing was made, and the walls of log cabins large enough to accommodate his family were put up by each member of the crew. A few days later, the little *Ark* sailed back to Pictou, to generate a wave of furious activity.

For the promised land was in sight; to make their way to the new haven of St. Ann's and to life in a community of godly-minded neighbours now became the obsession of each one of Norman McLeod's congregation. All winter long, work went on to build the small, double-ended open boats—seven in number—which were to carry the first body of the faithful to their new home. The *Ark* herself would also ply back and forth between St. Ann's and Pictou, but solely as the possession of Alexander Munro, Norman McLeod's chief backer and already a man of enterprise and means in the New World.

On May 20th, 1820, a brilliant day of sunshine, the little flotilla arrived inside the bar of St. Ann's, after a stormy passage across the Northumberland and Canso Straits, over the half-mile portage where the St. Peter's Canal now runs, and through the Bras d'Or Lakes.

It had been a curious pilgrimage for Norman McLeod and his followers, all the way from Scotland, for Pictou had been only an interruption. Like so many fervidly religious expeditions, from that of the Pilgrim Fathers to the Doukhobour Sons of Freedom, it had been a flight from religious freedom, rather than an escape to it. It was freedom to persecute which their leaders unconsciously sought; not the freedom from persecution which had prompted earlier religious migrations. Satisfied at last with his security from worldly interruption, Norman McLeod set about the fashioning of a kingdom which, for all its aspects of piety and asceticism, was to be a tyranny of a size and scope without parallel in North America; a tyranny extending into every aspect of life, both public and private, of every living soul within a sizable and increasingly significant community.

All about him, from his house on the slopes above Black Cove, were the simple homesteads of his parishioners; Norman MacDonald, Squire MacLeod, and Hugh Matheson on the south shore of South Gut; Ronald Ross, Roderick MacKenzie and the Munro brothers along the north shore of the

North Gut, the latter occupying a little headland known then—and now—as Munro's Point. Today, standing on the site of Norman McLeod's house, one can still see his domain much as he did more than a century and a half ago; the names of his parishioners then are the names of district families today. The early success of the tiny colony was remarkable; with each passing week more settlers arrived, both from Scotland, attracted overseas by the letters of relatives, and from Pictou and the infant hamlet of Sydney to the South.

It was security, perhaps more of the mind and spirit than merely physical, that they sought and found. Here, within the limits of this beautiful bay, and stretching soon as far afield as the North River and Boulardarie, was a community in the New World closely paralleling the tight-knit atmosphere of the clan society of the old Highlands. Here every contact with the world outside was looked after by their patriarchal leader, here their traditional way of life, austere yet fulfilling, could be carried on free from the disturbing worldliness of alien and sinful and aggressive neighbours. Here the tedium and hardship of their everyday life could be enlivened by the thunder and lightning of Sunday pulpit performances which were always impressive, sometimes awesome; occasionally, terrifying. It was a way of life peculiarly appealing to a people with the attributes of the Highlanders, accustomed both to endure physical hardship and to accept the rule of a jealous Jehovah in Heaven and of his zealous and vengeful prophet on earth.

For Norman McLeod established himself from the beginning as a ruler of more than temporal power, and increasingly saw himself as a latter-day Biblical patriarch comparable to his favorite, Paul. He began to speak of himself simply as "Norman," and of his particular creed of preaching as "Normanism." For him, the years at St. Ann's were the fulfillment of a lifelong yearning for power, which he, consciously or otherwise, had always sublimated in a professed zeal to carry out the wishes of a Divine Father. First, to confirm his spiritual powers, he journeyed to a Scots parish in Caledonia, New York, where he qualified as a minister of the Presbyterian Church, thus at last earning the title of "Reverend" and the status of minister in a recognized church.

He joined the church for this reason, and this reason alone. As he set forth in a letter: "Being placed at a distance, I have never experienced the least restraint or control; otherwise I should never have thought of joining any clergy for all my life in the world." Now that his spiritual status was confirmed, he set about to establish his authority in other fields. He had himself made magistrate in 1823, and in 1827 secured a license as schoolmaster, giving him complete control of the schooling of parish children. He was now legally and constitutionally qualified to rule on every matter, material, moral or spiritual, affecting the lives of everyone in St. Ann's, old or young, and he set himself with unflagging zeal to do just that. For the next thirty years he was to exercise an absolute rule never equalled, before or since, in the New World.

◆ 4 ◆

The Fear of God

Reverend Norman McLeod's Colony

BY MODERN STANDARDS, the long rule of the Reverend Norman McLeod during "the great days" of St. Ann's is simply incomprehensible. By today's notions, for thirty years he made the colony a sort of hell on earth, ruthlessly quelling any signs of rival initiative, mercilessly denouncing the most innocent indications of normal human behaviour and punishing them with a cruel gusto that was positively sadistic. Yet by far the greater number of his parishioners not only bore their joyless existence with resignation, but remained passionately devoted to their scourging tyrant with a faith that even now, one hundred and fifty years later, moves the hardest heart.

For it is a mistake to apply the standards of today to life in a primitive wilderness colony of an early nineteenth-century people accustomed to austerity in every aspect of life, and to a rule, spiritual and temporal, of an exacting and unforgiving nature, maintained by punishments that seem incredibly harsh and vengeful to modern eyes. The obedience and submission demanded of the Normanites varied only in degree from that required of most Highland congregations by the dominie; the penalties inflicted were no more vicious than those in common usage in a brutal age which relied on the gallows, the whip, the pillory, and the stocks to maintain order and decorum.

Yet for all of that, there can be no question but that Norman McLeod changed, during the period of his stay in St. Ann's, from a leader to a ruler, from a latter-day Moses leading his flock toward a New World Promised Land to a Nero savouring to the fullest the exercise of absolute power. There can be no doubt but that he became in fact what he had always been potentially: a megalomaniac to whom power was everything. After years of interpreting the Word of God for his flock, he came ultimately to identify the Divine Intent with his own; what he wished, God conveniently desired. In short, he assumed the status of an earthly Jehovah, and all his actions, some of them of the most petty and malicious kind, were cloaked in the omnipotent majesty of God's will.

It is significant that during this period every one of his friends who had formed the original nucleus of his colony, and who had followed him from Scotland and then from Pictou, the men of substance and ability and learning, were all ostracized by him, and under circumstances of evident malice. John Munro, who had built a prosperous trading and shipbuilding enterprise in the little colony, beginning with his purchase of the *Ark*, was driven out of the church and into ostracism by Norman over some fancied slight.

Squire MacLeod, most loyal of Norman's old friends and, at this distance, by all odds the most engaging, was dealt with even more cruelly. One of his sons had the misfortune to fall in love with Mary, one of Norman's two daughters. Since the stern father allowed Mary not so much as a moment alone with Luther, the Squire's son, and treated her still as a child not yet entitled to such adult privileges as leaving the house without permission, the young man attempted to resolve the problem of communicating with his beloved by sending letters to her, delivered by his father, since the Squire frequently called at Norman's house.

This paternal indulgence was to be terribly punished. Norman found out about the arrangement, innocent enough in all conscience, and his wrath shook the little colony to its foundations. Not only was the Squire barred from his old friend's house, but he was denounced from the pulpit as a moral miscreant of the basest sort. He was publicly humiliated, even to a denunciation of his every relationship with wife, family, servants. He was driven from the church, cut off from dealing with all parishioners, banished from the school board which he had done so much to establish and encourage. Henceforth this good and kindly man, perhaps the single most steadfast and capable supporter Norman had possessed, was a broken shadow in the community to which he had rendered such service.

And so it went; one by one, all the men whose character and capacity exempted them from the servile submission rendered Norman by humbler parishioners were broken to Norman's will. John Fraser, a Justice of the Peace, was accused of every sort of moral deformity and driven from office to make way for Norman's new son-in-law, John

Ross, now Justice of the Peace. No rival, actual or potential, was to be tolerated; one by one every man of initiative, character and ability was forced to publicly knuckle under or, as most did, to leave the colony altogether. In the end, Norman had no friends; only worshippers were tolerated.

Today, the heart of this little domain can be reached by the road immediately behind the grounds and open-air stage of the Gaelic College. A few hundred yards from the highway, the road passes a huge, gnarled old apple tree on sloping ground to the left of the road, just past the fence-line of an open field. Under the tree are the field-stone foundations and the partially-filled basement of a sizable building: the remains of Norman McLeod's house.

Here, about 1830, his parishioners built Norman a big three-storey house with sawn lumber brought from Pictou. In the old manner, each man in the parish owed Norman a yearly portion of his labour or yield, and thus the minister was enabled to live comfortably, with his fields tilled by parish volunteers and his house run by a volunteer staff headed by a housekeeper.

The original home, a log cabin above the cove, had been quickly outgrown; by the time she was forty-three Norman's wife Mary had borne no fewer than ten children, of whom all but one survived to maturity, although a son, Bunyan, died in his twenty-first year. The sole exception, little Edward, died in his first year and lies buried [with Bunyan] in a grave on the hillside marked with an epitaph touching in its abruptness: "Short spring; endless autumn." [The MacLeod Pioneer Cemetery lies along the Cabot Trail, about five kilometres north from the Gaelic College.]

Not unnaturally, Mary McLeod was in poor health most of the time; worn out by childbearing and the vicissitudes of living in a succession of primitive places, she was also emotionally exhausted by the strain of living with a man who, though a loving husband according to his lights, accorded her little role beyond that of a bearer of offspring, and who dominated a household of repressed, resentful children. When Norman was away, fiddles played for dances behind the locked doors and shutters of the big house that stood here; none of the boys turned out well. Norman, it was whispered in the community, turned a blind eye to conduct in his own boys which he fiercely denounced in others; conduct which included smuggling forbidden liquor in from nearby St. Pierre.

Today this old house site is a lovely place, serene and sunlit; it is difficult to conceive of it as it once was, a centre of power and piety, of repression and reproof; the central bastion of a system of organized misery and malice and hatred that perpetuated the name of a Saviour who preached the gospel of Universal Love. This must have been a house of immense and unbearable unhappiness, for all the loveliness of its setting.

Tragically, Norman McLeod, a born leader and gifted with courage, determination and intelligence above most men, lacked the warm qualities which can endear such prodigies to lesser mortals. In all the stories that survive him, there is not one which reflects a trace of pity, a shred of humour. He was a product of his time and place, where there was precious little to laugh at and pity was a weakness in an environment that put emphasis on strength. The harshness of his rule, resented by men of spirit even then, is almost unbelievable to us now. The Sabbath was—and still is—observed strictly in all Presbyterian congregations, but in St. Ann's Norman's rules were unparalleled. Two boys who skated to church on a cold winter Sunday were made to cut a hole in the ice and throw their skates into it. The buckets on maple trees during the spring runoff had to be spilled, so that sap that ran out of the trees on the Holy Day was not turned to man's advantage. No meal could be cooked, no dish washed, no apple picked nor even a drink taken from a brook on a Sabbath, and Norman attended to every detail of this meticulous observance with a zeal that today would smack of sadism. What could be crueler than his terrible attack on his own wife, already in poor health and delicate state of nerves, when she had the audacity to wear to church a bonnet of a color other than black, which she had bought for herself in Sydney? She was publicly humiliated before the whole congregation by her husband, who denounced her in terms more apt to the Scarlet Woman of Babylon than to the mother of his ten children.

In his house here, Norman was once guilty of a punishment which rocked even his most unquestioning supporters. A purse was stolen from a St. Ann's home, and a neighbour's boy was suspected. He denied his guilt but, when threatened with being locked overnight in the graveyard, he confessed. Norman ordered an ear to be cropped from the culprit as punishment, and one of the faithful obediently cut off a part of the boy's ear. A week later a witness told of seeing the purse being taken through a window by an itinerant pedlar, who was caught and confessed. Faced with the odium of his congregation, Norman went during the night to visit the boy's father. Whatever passed between them was never made known, but the father subsequently refused the offer of a Sydney lawyer to seek restitution on his son's behalf because to do so would be to "go against God."

Yet this ogre could be solicitous of his parishioners' welfare, and was remembered by many of them as a sort of loving father. He was also a schoolteacher of outstanding ability, and the school he established, the foundation of which can still be seen in the tall grass of the little peninsula, was one of his most remarkable achievements. Before its construction, he had taught in his home and in the church, but always, however slender his resources in terms of equipment and space, he proved a masterly teacher of an incredible range of subjects, and his pupils were the equal of those of the best-endowed schools in the land. Attendance varied, but between 70 and 110 pupils of varying ages could generally be found under his tutelage. Discipline was strict, as was only to be expected, but only once did Norman exceed accepted bounds. On that occasion, infuriated by an attractive young girl in his class, he reached for his birch rod. The class held its breath, for it was an unwritten law that girls were never beaten; only boys. Isaac MacLeod, youngest son of the Squire, leaped up to the front of the class and snatched the other end of the rod. The terrified girl ran for her life out the open door, and after a prolonged tugging match young MacLeod wrenched the rod from Norman's grip and flung it to one side, before striding from the school. He never returned; his father, already alienated from the community, enrolled him in a school on Boularderie Island run by a notable husband-and-wife team from Scotland, Mr. and Mrs. Alexander Munro, no relation to the family at Munro's Point.

This school was conducted in English, contrasting with Norman's which was taught in the native Gaelic, and it was sponsored by a Ladies' Association in Edinburgh headed by Mrs. Isabella MacKay, devoted to the cause of educating the Scots settlers of Cape Breton. Inevitably, this rival school, the relaxed atmosphere of which contrasted sharply with his own, was bitterly resented by Norman, and he devoted endless abuse to it, its dedicated lady workers, and its inclusion of subjects other than the traditional classic syllabus. Norman nicknamed Alexander Munro "Smerky," and ridiculed his educational qualifications, but he clearly resented most of all the range of teaching aids made available to "Smerky," which contrasted with his own meager complement of books and slates. For all its undoubted austerity, there can be no question but that Norman's school turned out the better scholars, nor that he himself, for all his harshness, was a superb teacher who gave of himself unreservedly in encouraging and coaching any of his students who showed promise, or interest in improving their education.

The schoolhouse stood close by Norman's home, where in fact he had once also taught. A little further eastward stood the church, and today if one follows the road running through the property the site can be clearly seen, standing in a clearing to the south of the roadside. A cairn and plaque mark this place, and the foundations can still be seen, a rectangular pattern of mound and hollow running through the low grass on a level site standing immediately above the wooded bank that slopes down to the waters of Black Cove. It is still, today, as it must have been then, a site of notable beauty, yet it is difficult now to associate this deserted patch of grass, somnolent in the summer sunshine, with the vital and vibrant heart of a community that encompassed hundreds of square miles.

Here stood a truly memorable building, one of the most influential and celebrated churches in the history of Canada. The building itself was put up more than twenty years after the beginning of the community, the successor to the original little church first built here in 1822. Known fittingly as "The Big Church," the new structure was of frame construction on a fieldstone foundation. Although it had neither tower nor belfry, and looked from outside like an enormous barn, sixty feet long, forty feet wide and twenty feet high, with a double tier of windows, the Big Church boasted a full gallery, and was said to accommodate a congregation of twelve hundred. Looking at the relatively modest dimensions of the foundations today, such a capacity seems questionable, but whatever it may have been it proved totally inadequate to the multitudes who descended upon it to hear Norman preach. When weather permitted, as it usually did during the long summer season, services were held outside, with the congregation seated on the grassy hillside, but on less clement Sabbaths every inch of the church, its corridors and stairways, was packed with people, all come to hear Norman.

From as far away as Whycocomagh, far up the Bras d'Or Lakes, they came, starting their long journey on Friday so as to be on time for the Sunday services, and returning to their homes early the following week after a grueling trip in primitive conditions. Along both sides of St. Ann's Bay they journeyed from far-off Cape Smokey, over winding mountain trails that today would deter the strongest hiker. From North River and the North Shore, from Boularderie and Baddeck, the congregations set out, whole families of them, all headed for the great, stark church which once stood in this now-deserted spot.

They did not come as individual and independent celebrants, in the accepted Presbyterian tradition which made each man his own judge, before God; Norman would have none of that. In his view, his parishioners were too depraved to enjoy admission to the rites of the church of God, and he barred men and women from communion and children from baptism. Nor was it mere piety alone which brought such incredible numbers to Norman's church; rather it was the experience, one of the rare joys permitted in this God-fearing community, of hearing preaching the like of which they had never heard before, performed—and that is the operative word—by a master of the art.

Here in this sunlit place, where today the silence is broken only by the occasional bumblebee busy about his rounds, hundreds once cowered in delicious fright before the whips and scorpions—a favorite phrase—of Norman's tongue. Here, enjoying a rare sense of community after a week of workaday isolation, Norman's scattered parishioners could forget the tedium and hardship of existence in the exaltation of scourging the devil and all his works, salted from time to time by the savour of evil-doing rather closer to home. For Norman was a preacher who named names and cited instances; his parishioners were never left in any doubt as to the identity of his victims. None was spared, not even, as has been noted, Norman's own dutiful wife; indeed, people of enterprise or standing could be sure that their moment would inevitably come, when they would be denounced in scathing terms before the assembled congregation of their neighbours, for any of a vast range of sins, of which "false pride" seems to have been most prevalent.

But these public humiliations could stem from the most unlikely incidents. A story is still cherished in the district concerning Mrs. Murdoch MacLeod, who one day noticed that a man rafting logs down the bay had been caught by wind and tide and was being blown helplessly out toward the open sea. The unfortunate man was one whom Norman had driven from the church, denying its privileges to him and instructing his parishioners to ostracize him and his family. In the crisis, Mrs. MacLeod reproached her husband and sons for sitting by and allowing a man to drift into danger simply because of his status as a church exile, and stung by her sharp tongue, they got into their boat and went out and rescued him.

Next Sunday Murdoch MacLeod was the subject of a tirade of abuse for disregarding the strict commandments of his pastor and leader, in extending assistance to a man who had been declared an outcast. In a fury of resentment, Murdoch gathered all the members of his household about him and stalked from the church, never to return.

As the years wore on, there were many such; one by one, men of initiative and intelligence were ostracized by the growing tyranny of a man whom they had originally admired and respected, and the growing demagoguery of his behaviour. For Norman increasingly played upon the innate resentment of the Celt for those about him who set themselves up as in any way superior—either by enterprise, manner or hard work. To the dour Highlander, there was something grimly satisfying in seeing such pushy neighbours brought low by their minister's cruel tongue; a satisfaction relished despite the knowledge that he himself might be next to feel that verbal whip about his shoulders.

Even Norman's Pictou friend and chief supporter, John Gordon, was cruelly ridiculed for placing an epitaph on the tombstone of a member of his family "out of keeping with his low and obscure circumstance."

The moment came, eventually and inevitably, to Norman McDonald, for fifteen years Norman's staunch friend and supporter, and one of the founding fathers of the little community, who had followed Norman all the way from Assynt and had, in a very real sense, devoted his life to furthering the work of a man he revered above all others. McDonald could not stomach the growing tyranny, the demagoguery that affronted the intelligence and increasingly identified the Lord's will with that of Norman McLeod. He, too, was driven out into the wilderness, and left the little settlement he had helped to found. After years of exile, he returned to die, but his family never came back.

Curiously, Norman saved the full fury of his scorn and abuse for his fellow Presbyterians; he viewed members of other Protestant and Catholic congregations with tolerance and good will, although he considered that their teachings were in error. But nothing could exceed the contempt and hatred in which he held his fellow ministers of the Presbyterian church in Cape Breton, "the very tag and tail of preaching." A sample survives, in his letter to an old college friend, the Reverend A. McLeod: "You were never by nature but a mere simpleton, or two-thirds of an idiot, and your false conversion, scraps of philosophy, fragments of divinity, painted parlour, dainty table, sable surtout, curled cravat, ponderous purse, big belly, poised pulpit, soft and silly spouse, the acclamation of fanatics and formalists, the association of kindred plagiarists and impostors, your seared conscience and a silent God have all conspired, no wonder, poor man, to turn your mind to total forgetfulness and your head to eternal dizziness...."

Even today, the words drip with envy and malice; when an old friend in faraway Scotland received such treatment, what might not a nearby rival expect? Hundreds upon hundreds packed Norman's church, Sunday after Sunday, to find out, and they were not disappointed. As their leader grew older he seemed to gain in fire and eloquence with each passing year, and by 1848, when he faced his ultimate crisis in this place, he was entering his seventieth year.

The immediate cause was a freak frost, coming in late spring after all wheat and potatoes had been planted, and which destroyed not only the crop on which the community intended to survive next winter, but the priceless seed grain needed to engender future crops. Coming on top of a series of poor yield years, this disaster meant famine, unless supplies could be purchased from outside.

This natural disaster caught the little community at a particularly vulnerable moment. Norman, despite his overbearing harshness in bench and pulpit, was a careful, dedicated and hardworking shepherd to his flock. At St. Ann's nobody ever got into trouble with gamblers or bootleggers, nobody was victimized by the swindlers of one kind and another who preyed upon so many gullible settlers in communities nearby. Anyone could come to Norman for help or advice; he wrote letters for the illiterate, counseled worried parishioners on matters of law and commerce. It was the guidance and leadership of this strong man which bound the community together, giving its people a security that was lacking in other similar settlements, and imparting the cooperative spirit and sense of community which was remarked on by Judge Thomas Chandler Haliburton when he visited here during his travels through the raw new territory of Nova Scotia. "Its inhabitants are Scots dissenters, the most sober, industrious and orderly settlement on the island, and have a pastor of their own to whose exertions and vigilance the character of the people is not a little indebted."

The difficulty with the tight little self-sufficient society of fishermen-farmers which Norman McLeod had consciously founded and fostered was that it depended entirely for its livelihood upon its ability to grow its own food. In an area where the land was shallow and the Atlantic weather could be fickle, this was a dangerously narrow base upon which to support a constantly growing community; a poor catch, a poor crop, and the whole settlement faced extinction.

What was needed was another iron in the fire, another source of livelihood independent of Nature's vagaries. Such a potential lifesaver had been developing across the North Gut from Norman's house, on the holding of the enterprising Munro family.

Still known locally as Munro's Point, this little piece of land juts into the North Gut near the mouth of the North River, and it is easily reached today by the Cabot Trail which winds around past the Gaelic College and skirts the shores of the Gut. It is now privately owned, and a summer home stands on the property, with a long sloping drive running down from the highway. Here one can still see the traces of the shipways and artisans' buildings which once stood here, and the shore still slopes gently into deep water, making the site ideal for the building and launching of ships. On this point the enterprising John Munro first settled, and here he established a store, a shipyard, and a lumberyard. Later, he moved his shipbuilding operations to the nearby Shipyard Point, and built two gristmills at the mouth of nearby streams, the ruins of which can still be seen. Old residents still treasure stories of the first polling booth set up in the Munro store, one side for Tories and the other for Grits, with a big barrel of rum between from which each party organizer, dipper in hand, rewarded each supporter as he voted.

From the very beginning, Munro's business thrived. Britain, recovering from her titanic struggle with Napoleon's continental tyranny, was desperate for ships and timber; St. Ann's could supply both. By the British Navigation Act, the North American colonies enjoyed a monopoly of trade with the West Indies; quickly, John Munro built vessels for this lucrative trade. More ships were needed for the Labrador and Banks fisheries; John Munro built some himself, and helped finance others. Here, on this point, now so silent, was developed a thriving commercial enterprise, which employed some of Norman's people as shipwrights and fitters, others as lumberjacks. It infused money into the settlement by buying timber from settlers, and brought them goods on which to spend it at the Munro store; goods brought in by Munro's own little ships. An attempt was made by others to emulate Munro's venture, but with limited success. A 90-ton vessel, the *Maria*, was built by Norman's sons, John and Murdoch, in 1838, but another son, Donald, who was supposed to take ship and lumber cargo to Glasgow and sell them, and return with the proceeds, simply sailed away and did not return. His absconding did not deter the brothers from building other ships, engaging in other ventures, some of which were rumoured to involve smuggling, and other men built small vessels for the coasting and Indies trades, but nobody approached the scope of the Munro operations. By the 1840s, as many as seven ships a season were arriving from Britain to load lumber from the Munro yard in St. Ann's, apart from that shipped in Munro's own vessels.

In short, the Munro enterprise became a vital part of the St. Ann's economy, and its best hope for future success. It was, therefore, a disastrous blow for the community that in the very year of its crushing crop failure, Munro should have fallen afoul of Norman McLeod's wrath, apparently over the alleged importation of some West Indian rum aboard a Munro ship. In high dudgeon, Norman ordered everyone in the community to have nothing to do with Munro or with any of his enterprises; they were not to buy his goods, sell him their lumber, offer him their work. Such an edict was fatal, both to Munro's business and to the community which it sustained; Munro was forced into receivership, his whole complex operation ground to a halt, and McLeod's starving parishioners were deprived of the income they would need to buy supplies from the outside. It was a terrible, fateful decision, yet for all its seeming folly at this distance in time, one cannot but be impressed both with the resolute integrity of the leader who gave the suicidal order and the unquestioning faith of his followers in the face of veritable starvation.

In the event, Munro's two sons, Hugh and Daniel, were later able to resurrect their father's shattered business, and Norman managed, after desperate entreaty, to receive a meager supply of flour from the Nova Scotia government which enabled his famished people to survive the winter, but it was now clear to him that his little community could not weather another such storm. The timber trade to Britain had eased off, the West Indian shipping had been opened up to European competition; the situation in St. Ann's was grim indeed, and the challenge to Norman McLeod, now in vigorous old age, was more urgent than anything he had ever had to face in his prime. By depriving his people of their opportunity to subsist, at least in part, on the trading enterprise of the ostracized Munro, he had made himself wholly responsible both for their present survival and their future prospects.

Norman in this crisis turned to prayer, and it would not have taken a particularly religious man to see the workings of Divine Providence in the solution that presented itself. For at the height of the famine a letter arrived from Norman's prodigal son, Donald, who had run away with the family ship and cargo seven years before. He had emigrated to Australia and set himself up as editor of a newspaper in that booming new continent, and he wrote his father now urging him to bring his parishioners to this land of promise, where they could establish themselves in conditions far easier than those prevailing in frostbitten St. Ann's Bay. This chance letter, and the prospects it opened out before him, inspired Norman to undertake a pilgrimage, the story of which, even today, stirs the imagination of everyone who encounters it.

◆ 5 ◆

The Flowers of the Forest

From St. Ann's to Waipu ◆ 1849-1866

It IS CURIOUS TODAY to consider how a letter, and subsequent communications in the spring and summer of 1849, from a prodigal runaway, could have led to the virtual depopulation of a substantial part of Cape Breton. It is explicable only in terms of the immense stature of a single man, the Reverend Norman McLeod.

Whatever his arrogance, however harsh and tyrannous his rule, there can be no question but that it was he, and he alone, who had imparted a sense of communal identity to the straggling settlements of St. Ann's; he was the shepherd, they the trusting flock. But the crisis that arose out of the famine of 1848, and the brooding anguish and crushing sense of responsibility that settled on him, transformed Norman yet again. Where he had been a tyrant, demanding complete subservience on pain of expulsion, he was transformed in the twilight of his life into a benevolent patriarch, dedicated to the task of leading his people to a new and better life, again a Moses seeking for his followers a haven in a far-off Promised Land.

It is this period of his life that most of Norman's followers liked to recall in after years; the parental concern, the solicitude, the strengthening faith that uplifted the minds and hearts of hundreds of sorely-distressed men and women. For this move, after thirty years of residence in a homeland carved out, at fearful cost, in a primitive land, was infinitely more difficult than the initial voyage to Nova Scotia from a Scotland which had no place for them, or of the subsequent transfer, after so brief a stay, from Pictou to St. Ann's. For now there were many among them who had families of young children, unable to face so long and arduous a voyage. There were others, too, who had found happiness and fulfillment here, who were proud of their farmland holdings, carved out on the first land they had ever owned themselves, and so were reluctant to abandon everything, however dismal their present lot, for the uncertain prospects of an unknown and faraway land.

Indeed, there can be no question but that, if their leader had not determined to move, the stubborn Scots of St. Ann's would have held on, despite trade recessions and bad crops, and somehow scraped through. But Norman could see that, to do so, meant of necessity an increasing reliance on trade, with all the resultant disruption of their established, self-sufficient way of life. There would be growing numbers of new arrivals in the colony, of men whose background and attitudes must inevitably have clashed with that of his Highland parishioners. It would mean a loosening of the strong ties which had held the settlement together for so long, through such difficulties, and at a time when he himself, who had led them so long, must look forward to a progressive lessening of his own powers of leadership. Here, it seemed to him, was the clear path, miraculously made clear to them by the chance letter of his prodigal son, by which the men and women of St. Ann's could maintain their communal identity in a new land whose many amenities, as described to them in letters, were in such contrast to the hardships they now faced. He turned himself to the task of forming his flock about him, and of bracing it for the terrible ordeal it must face, with a courage and a zeal and humility worthy of the Biblical prophets in whose role he had once affected to cast himself.

Each family, each member of families, had individual decisions to make: to go or to stay. For all who elected to go, Norman furnished encouragement and assistance and advice: dispose of property, collect portable belongings, prepare supplies. In a flurry of activity, St. Ann's and the settlements for miles around became a sort of disturbed ants' nest of hectic scurryings and desperate activity, as people, who until a short time ago had never so much as heard of Australia, prepared themselves to travel more than twelve thousand miles to its unknown shores. There was a sort of eagerness, especially among the young, at the prospect before them of arrival in a new and unknown world, but for their elders, and even more for all of those, old and young, who had determined to stay where they were, this was a time of deep and abiding sadness, a prospect, like that of approaching death, of irretrievable loss and sorrow.

Of chief concern, of course, was the construction of ships to transport so large a body of people so vast a distance. Here in St. Ann's a party of a hundred and forty people, nearly forty of whom were children, had determined to go, and accordingly a vessel capable of carrying them had to be built, but this was by no means the full extent of the exodus to the Antipodes. Nearly seven hundred men and women were to follow Norman to his remote new colony, and ships to carry them—the *Highland Lass*, the *Gertrude*, the *Spray*, the *Breadalbane*, the *Ellen Lewis*—were being built and fitted out in nearby ports around Cape Breton. The very scope of the pilgrimage, the multitude of the people and the immensity of the distance they had to travel, the hardships and uncertainties they faced, is eloquent testimony to the quality and magnetism of their elderly but indomitable leader.

At St. Ann's today, along the road between the overgrown foundations of Norman's home and the site of the Big Church, a little trackway leads off to the southward near the edge of a grove of trees. Although heavily overgrown, it is recognizable as a ramped and leveled road, and it can still be followed down through the spruce woods toward the shores of Black Cove, passing beneath the plateau of the church site, and emerging on the mirror-like waters of a sheltered cove, landlocked and protected from most of the winds that blow. A sandy beach slopes off into the dark water, and high bluffs and wooded banks provide a screen against the prevailing westerlies. Here, where the *Ark*'s crew had originally landed, its survivors now prepared a much greater vessel to bear them away yet again.

On the sandy beach reached by several trackways, whose ramped remains can still be traced and followed today, cut timber from the nearby forest was assembled. Black birch, close-grained and more durable even than oak—the favourite of shipbuilders of the time, particularly for below-waterline work—grew, and still grows, abundantly here. One can still see where lumber and other supplies were skidded down to the beach; other timber would be rafted round in a tow of small boats. Here on this little beach Neil and Roderick McGregor, master shipbuilders and the pride of the colony's shipyards, laid the keel and set up the frames in June 1849 for the great ship *Margaret* that was to carry so many so far. A fine, sturdy, heavily-timbered vessel of 246 burthen with slight sheer and fine bows, she can best be appreciated today by a model of her [made and donated by William Ross, St. Ann's] which can be seen at the Gaelic College nearby. She was rigged as a three-masted barque, with yards for square sails on fore and main masts only.

On this fine ship every able-bodied man lavished every hour he could manage, and she grew rapidly, but there was no scrimping of quality for speed. Her iron work was carefully wrought and galvanized, and by the summer of 1850 the ship's hull was completed, painted, and launched. Here, however, came the difficulty that nearly wrecked the entire venture. The men of the community had fashioned everything that could be made with the work of their own hands, but now they needed money to buy the sails and cordage for rigging which could only be purchased outside the community, and there were no funds left them. All summer, all fall, all winter the unfinished ship swung to her moorings in the little cove, while the hopes of the desperate men and women ashore languished with each passing month.

Yet now, across this somber scene there flashed a shaft of romance, like sunshine against a threatening backdrop of thundercloud; a romance whose warmth and tenderness is all the more poignant against the prevailing darkness.

In that anxious autumn of 1850, a barque from Aberdeen arrived late in the season to load lumber, and was trapped for the winter in St. Ann's Bay by an early freeze-up. Here young second officer, Hugh Anderson, met and fell in love with Margaret, Norman McLeod's lovely and vivacious twenty-two-year-old daughter. During the winter he disappeared from the ship and could not be found despite sustained searches. It was presumed he had fallen through a crevasse in the harbour ice and the following spring the ship sailed without him, but no sooner had the vessel safely disappeared over the horizon than Hugh Anderson appeared from the woodland cabin where he had been hidden, and supplied with food, by his devoted Margaret. Both lovers knew that Norman would never have consented to a marriage which would have carried his daughter away to Aberdeen, but now they hoped to gain approval for a marriage which would take them with Norman's followers to Australia.

Norman accepted Hugh Anderson's offer to help rig the ship, and to act as navigator for the long voyage, but ignored the young man's plea for his daughter's hand. In the end, however, love was to triumph; two years later, in far-off New Zealand, the young couple were married.

Whatever Norman may have thought of it, the romance of these attractive young people captivated the little colony, and they named their new ship *Margaret*. It was a fortunate omen; that same spring a visiting United Empire Loyalist named John Robertson arrived in the course of a trip through the island, admired the McLeod home and property and bought them for three thousand dollars; enough to purchase the precious sails and rigging so long awaited. By autumn of the same year the *Margaret* was rigged, stored, and ready to sail.

In the little colony, thirty-two years of intensive settlement were now nearing an end. Norman turned over the keys of the Big Church to the Free Presbyterian Church of Nova Scotia, which he had so often abused. It was to stand, without a pastor, for nearly five years, but its beautifully arched windows, its four broad entrances, its great gallery around three sides, and its floor sloped upward from the pulpit, were still to be the wonder of visiting clergymen, and enhance the memory of its awesome founder. The women who were departing for Australia had long since finished preparing their food to survive the torrid temperatures of their long passage through the tropics. Potatoes were dried and shredded before being wrapped in birchbark, and the dried codfish that was the other great staple of life was packed in the same manner. Meat was pickled, yeastless bread and biscuit stowed in waterproof containers; some even experimented with evaporated milk.

The final moment came on October 28th, 1851:

a glorious day of sunshine and flaming autumn colours that made the steep headlands of St. Ann's a gorgeous backdrop to the jewel-like waters of the bay. It was just such another day as that which had first entranced the men of the little *Ark* thirty-two years before; it is ironic that Norman's first, and last, sight of St. Ann's should have been at its moments of greatest beauty.

The Big Church site at St. Ann's today is, as it was then, in a grassy clearing below a gently-sloping hillside. Standing there now it is easy to picture the place as it was on that autumn day more than a century ago; the passing years have altered the landscape only in minor detail. Here on this hillside assembled everyone who could make the journey; old and young, all of them traveled the long miles to take their farewell of neighbours, friends, and children who were journeying far away. For most of them who were staying behind, it was to be a final parting; they were never to see again those faces which had long been so familiar. It was a parting of particular poignance for the elderly, who were bidding farewell to sons and daughters who were traveling literally a world away, and for younger men and women who were taking leave of sisters and brothers whom they would never look upon again.

Silent in their sadness, the travelers, and their friends and families who were staying behind, joined in Norman McLeod's last service at St. Ann's. Tall and spare, his white hair blown by the breeze, Norman stood where the road now runs, facing his enormous congregation. The hillside was covered with people; below, on the sunlit waters of the cove, the *Margaret* swung impatiently to her moorings, her sails bent and ready.

His voice breaking with emotion at times, Norman presided in his usual black gown, in a service which was his final leavetaking of his St. Ann's parishioners. Blown by the wind, his voice yet rose harsh and strong in his final blessing. It was, said those who took part in it, Norman's greatest sermon. In it, he made clear to all what was embodied in this solemn moment. Those who were setting out "for the Destined Land" were dedicated to their great pilgrimage, to their tryst with destiny past unknown perils. Those who stayed were comforted, but were challenged in spirit, too.

After the service, the travelers embarked, and Norman moved among the throngs of his remaining parishioners for the last time. It was as he appeared at this moment, this indomitable old man, his eyes moist, his powerful frame stooped by the years, yet gentle now in voice and handshake as he took his last leave, that his people remembered him best, when they themselves grew old.

Late that afternoon the *Margaret* began her voyage, dropping down the bay before a brisk westerly and falling tide, past the hillsides black with people, past the ruins of Fort Dauphin to the open sea. To the dour Scots watching, it was clear that they were losing their leader, the heart of their community, the centre of their life's concern for more than thirty years. For most of them, it was the end of everything they had ever known, and it wrung from these least demonstrative of people a wailing lamentation the like of which this bay had never known.

And then she was gone; it was all over, and an era had ended.

"And on the mere the wailing died away."

THE SUBSEQUENT WANDERINGS and experiences of the *Margaret* and her passengers were followed by those who stayed in St. Ann's, in letters received by infrequent post from the other end of the world. They told of the safe arrival of the *Margaret* at Adelaide and then Melbourne, and of her sale there.

But the rest of the news was tragic. Melbourne was a boomtown where conditions made those of wicked Pictou appear like the atmosphere of a kindergarten. The refugees found themselves living in the fearful squalor of Canvastown, a sort of tent city on the outskirts of Melbourne. Some of the younger men went off to seek their fortunes at Ballarat and Bendigo, where the new goldfields were the magnet for adventurers from every quarter of the world. There was no law; bush rangers prowled the roads at night, robbing and killing all whom they came across. All but the Reverend Norman McLeod, that is. The seventy-two-year-old Norman, lost in the bush with night coming on, was captured by a band of these desperadoes. In contrast with their usual practice, they spared his life, although he had no money, presumably out of respect for his clerical collar. They may well have regretted their soft-heartedness in inviting this white-haired Scot to share their campfire for the night; it is said that he lectured them for hours on their wicked ways, and on the inevitable consequences, so that it was with considerable relief that they gave him back his horse and sent him on his way in the morning.

But worse than the lack of law and order was the lack of hygiene. Conditions in the stinking heat of Canvastown were unspeakable, and inevitably typhoid broke out. It raced through the camp of the Highland emigrants like wildfire; within weeks it had taken a fearful toll, and among the dead were the three younger sons of Norman McLeod.

Once again, it was clear to Norman that his little colony would literally perish if no move was made, and it was fortunate that another large group of his supporters from Nova Scotia had just arrived in the *Highland Lass* from Baddeck. With the proceeds of the sale of this vessel a coasting schooner, the *Gazelle*, was bought and fitted out. In this little ship nineteen of Norman's parishioners from St. Ann's embarked, together with ninety of the *Highland Lass* passengers from the Bras d'Or, and left the gold-boom economy of Australia, with all its promises of quick riches and its perils of quick death, for the more appealing prospect of New Zealand, where a wise governor was building a stable community based on agriculture.

Norman followed on the next trip with the balance of his family and others who wished to settle with him, and they established themselves at the mouth of the Waipu River north of Auckland, on the North Island of New Zealand. They chose this place in preference to the much better lands offered them at Hawke Bay, because it reminded them of their old homes at St. Ann's Bay in far-off Cape Breton: a wooded foreshore, rising into high hills, enclosing deep, sheltered bays. Here their lion-hearted old leader settled them into much the sort of community they had known all their lives.

And here, in March 1866, weary and worn-out at last at the age of eighty-six, he took his final leave of them as they stood about his deathbed: "Children, children, look to yourselves, the world is mad."

◆ 6 ◆

The Gentle Giant

Angus MacAskill ◆ 1825-1863

ENGLISHTOWN, the community on the south shore of St. Ann's settled originally by discharged British soldiers and so named because it was the only settlement in the area which did not "have the Gaelic," is today the only part of old St. Ann's which retains a distinct communal identity. Thousands of visitors pass through it each summer on their way to the little ferry which provides such a pleasant interlude on a journey around the scenic Cabot Trail. About a mile west of the ferry wharf the summer tourists stream past the weather-beaten wreck of an old house tottering on a knoll above the south side of the road. [This description was written around 1975. Today, the homestead is the site of the Giant MacAskill Museum.] None of the passersby, and indeed few enough of local residents, pay it any heed, but this roofless ruin, with its sagging walls and empty windows, is the last visible link with the Cape Breton Giant, a colossal man whose size and strength were once renowned throughout the world.

There is still a usable driveway leading into

the abandoned property; enough, at least, in which to park a car, and to provide a grassy footpath which leads upward through the spruce bush which now crowds in on every side. The ruined house, in the last stages of dereliction, is the standard frame two-storey structure common to the region, and it belonged to an uncle of the Giant, but the real interest of the site lies elsewhere.

The pathway, all that remains of a once-broad farm road, winds upward through pretty wooded land; a little way above the house it opens into a lovely clearing, still level and grass-covered in the sea of trees. Here [circa 1975] stand the foundations of the Giant's home; the grass-grown mounds which are all that remain of what was once the most famous house in all Cape Breton, home of a man whose name was legendary throughout the English-speaking world.

This pleasant place, still charming although its once-superb view over the bay is now choked with trees, was the home of Angus MacAskill, an enormous young man whose size and prodigious strength made him a notable celebrity in the middle of the nineteenth century. There is a museum dedicated to him nearby. His grave in the village cemetery is a celebrated tourist site, and the memory of his feats imparts a distinctive ambiance to many parts of the shore where he lived and worked and wrought his marvels. But it is here, in this sunlit, sheltered place, forgotten by the outside world, where his presence is still almost a tangible thing. For this clearing once rang to his great axe; this road he trod, winter and summer, most of the years of his life, and within the compass of that moldering foundation he grew from budding boyhood to magnificent maturity.

To begin with, of course, this was his father's home. Norman MacAskill, a stout man, five feet nine inches tall, bought the cabin and clearing from Donald MacAulay in 1831, and moved into it his large family. Although there had been thirteen children born to Norman and his wife Christina, several of them died in infancy, as was normal for that primitive place and time; one son, Angus, had been born at the family homestead in Harris, in the Hebridean Islands, in 1825 and even as a six-year-old was still smaller than the other children. And there were lots of children about; this deserted place then was alive with them, for in addition to the large MacAskill brood there were the nine children of neighbour Murdock MacLeod and the four children of young Duncan MacLeod. It was a lasting legacy these hardy Scots bequeathed to their new home and to this day the population of Englishtown is dominated by MacLeods and MacAskills.

Unlike the majority of the children west and north of them, the MacAskill children did not go to the school run by their redoubtable minister, the Reverend Norman McLeod, although it was to his church that all of them belonged. They attended instead the school run by Alexander Munro on Boularderie Island and in all likelihood they boarded there, coming home only for weekends. It was a long walk from Englishtown, up over 800-foot Kelly's Mountain and down again to the Great Bras d'Or on the other side, with a long boat ride to Boularderie Island, but there was no other way, and given enough time, any hardy youngster of the day could manage it at holiday time.

It was to Munro's school that young Angus MacAskill went, along with an older brother, and they made up part of a class of pupils of all ages from five to seventeen years, averaging about thirty-seven in number. Angus seems to have been an exemplary pupil, and an attendance record still surviving shows that the ten-year-old boy had a perfect attendance record for the school year of 1834. A mark of one hundred and forty consecutive schooldays without once being absent or late for classes was no small feat in a time when bad weather, particularly in the winter, must have proved a tremendous problem for a young boy with so far to walk after weekends or holidays. It cost his father two pounds ten shillings—in those days money was tallied both in dollars and pounds sterling—for six months of instruction and probably board for young Angus, school records show, and it can be appreciated that spending even so small a sum was a difficult matter for the fathers of families as large as the MacAskills and MacLeods. Alexander Munro, Angus' teacher, earned a salary of sixty pounds a year, with living allowance of seven shillings a week for board, lodging and laundry, and for a graduate of King's College, in Aberdeen, it was certainly something less than a princely salary.

Certainly he served a large and growing number of students. By 1838 fully half the Englishtown population of two hundred and three persons were children of school age, and descendants of the children he taught are there to this day—MacAulay,

MacDonald, MacIver, MacLeod, Campbell, Ferguson, Fraser, Kerr, Matheson, Morrison and Sutherland—a glance at the St. Ann's Bay telephone directory shows how little basic population stock has changed in more than a century and a half. In 1838 there were twenty-three heads of households who were farmers, two were merchants, two carpenters, a blacksmith, a weaver, a fisherman and a sailor.

By his second year in school, young Angus MacAskill was beginning to grow; already he was larger than his schoolfellows, and could thrash anyone in a fight. Mostly it appears to have been good-natured wrestling, however; Angus seems to have been blessed with a placid disposition and a good control of his temper, qualities which were to be displayed throughout his life. By the time he was fourteen he was huge, and still growing at an amazing rate; well over six feet, he was nicknamed Gille Mor by his schoolmates, which is Gaelic for "Big Boy." About this time, too, people began to talk about his amazing strength, and it is from this period that the legend of the Cape Breton Giant really begins.

At fourteen, for example, Angus went ashore at North Sydney from a fishing boat on which he was crewing during the summer school break, and went with his shipmates to a dance. Not having any shoes, he sat near the door and watched the dancers. Details of the story vary, but apparently at some time during the evening one of the local young men danced his way over to Angus and taunted him about his bare feet, and subsequently on his circuits of the floor he went out of his way to step on the Big Boy's bare toes. The second time this happened Angus stood up menacingly, but was restrained from fighting by those next to him, but the young tormentor lacked the sense to avoid another confrontation. The next time around he trod heavily on Angus' foot—and nearly died as a consequence. Angus landed only one blow, a tremendous right hand to the side of the head, but it hurled his antagonist into the middle of the floor and laid him out unconscious. He remained unconscious for so long that it was feared he might be dead but eventually he was brought around. When the St. Ann's crew returned aboard they found Angus on his knees by his bunk, praying that he had not killed a man.

It was probably the last time that anyone, drunk or sober, ever challenged the burgeoning young giant to a fight of any kind; from that time on the legends are of feats of strength, not of brawls; no man in his right mind would care to mix it with a man of such prodigious strength.

And prodigious it was; there is scarcely a part of the Englishtown area which has not its particular legend of a feat of strength by the Big Boy. Here, near the clearing where his home once stood, was the hole for the family sawpit. Here planks were ripsawn from logs by two-handed saws, with one man standing in the pit over which stood the two sawhorses on which the logs were laid, and the top sawyer handling the saw above. Here Norman MacAskill and two of his sons found themselves unable to lift a particularly huge log onto the sawhorses—a straight lift of nearly six feet. At the dinner table the father had scolded Angus for not being around to give them a hand, and after the short noon rest period he ordered Angus to come along with his brothers and lend a hand. Angus told him that it was not necessary, that he had already, by himself, put the log up on the horses. His dumbfounded father saw for himself that the log was indeed now in position, but couldn't believe that even Angus had not needed assistance from someone. Flushed at the rebuke, Angus rolled the heavy log off the horses, with one hand, like some sapling, then bent down and with a single heave of his tremendous shoulders he lifted the log back into position.

It was the most convincing demonstration possible to Angus' father; more than anything else, it convinced him that his son was not just another big, strong boy, but a prodigy, and moreover one destined to grow into a veritable giant. Now began a necessary but difficult and expensive task; the reconstruction of the family home to house the growing dimensions of the young giant. Father and sons now set to work to raise the ceilings of the kitchen and living room downstairs and the roof above the bedrooms upstairs. For some reason, the front door was left at its original size, so that for the rest of his days Angus had always to stoop deeply to enter his home, but once inside he was comfortable enough, with room everywhere, except under the slope of the eaves, in which to stand upright. A huge bed and a large chair, both of which survive today in the museum, were also made at this time; the bed, eight feet long and sprung with ropes instead of string, proved in the long run to be not quite large enough when Angus came into his full growth.

Naturally enough, the giant's home came to be talked about throughout the district, along with the outsize furniture it housed. Timber-framed, it was covered with clapboards of wide pine nailed over sheets of birchbark, which acted as insulation. It had a central hallway from which a flight of stairs led up to two large upper bedrooms, one for boys on one side, the other side for girls, with the ground floor given over to kitchen, parlour, and parents' bedroom. A big stone chimney ran up the centre of the house, serving big fireplaces in kitchen and parlour and warming the upper bedrooms through which it passed. Cooking, in these days before stoves became popular, was done at the open fireplace, served by an iron bar or crane from which hung six pothooks, three long, three short. Long ones carried pots close to the fire, the short ones kept pots away from the greatest heat.

The house, magnificently sited, was still a wonder in the area long after the Giant himself had passed away, and it survived up to recent times. There are men in Englishtown today who can recall seeing the house standing derelict, still with its enormous bed inside, but it fell into disrepair during the Depression years and gradually melted away, its timbers and fittings being looted by neighbours to use in building new houses and barns. Today, only the grassgrown foundations survive standing above the shallow basement, but the house lives on in yellowing photographs, and in the folklore of the whole eastern seaboard.

On the hillside behind the house site is the little field, now treegrown and abandoned, where Angus displayed again his growing strength as a young teenager. Here his father had undertaken to plough the field within a set period of time to win a bet from a neighbour. One of the two horses hitched to the plough went lame, but young Angus came to the rescue. The horse was taken out of the span and the boy took its place, settling his enormous shoulders into the padded horsecollar and pulling his full weight of the load with the remaining horse beside him. With his father at the traces and plough handles, away the old team went, man and horse hitched in equal effort. According to legend, the bet would have been won, too, had not Mrs. MacAskill intervened; happening to see her son linked in this way in a horse harness, the indignant mother quickly put a stop to things and subjected both father and son to such a tongue-lashing that Angus was glad to pay the ten-dollar bet to the neighbour to end the matter.

Many of Angus' feats, which are still told today, centre about the shingle beach immediately to the east of the remains of Fort Dauphin, the old French fort which commanded the harbour entrance. Here fishermen could launch their boats right into the narrow channel and the open sea without having to sail or row the long and tedious distance down the bay, which would be necessary if launching from Englishtown itself. As a young man, Angus had a boat adapted for his great size; ballasted before the mast to offset his four-hundred-pound bulk in the stern, and with a forty-foot mast which he could step and unstep himself, as easily as if handling a broomstick, to the great delight of onlookers. He tossed anchors about like so many paperweights; a three-hundred-pound American skipper, himself a huge man and proud of his strength, who challenged Angus to a wrestling match, was heaved right over a woodpile ten feet high and twelve feet wide.

The fishermen's beach is today just as it was a century and a half ago, and is still used to beach boats occasionally, although most fishermen have inboard power and keep their boats afloat in the shelter of Englishtown harbour inside the bay.

Behind the sloping beach of gravel and stones lies a large brackish pond or lagoon, part of a characteristic formation called a "barrachois," as the Acadians named it. Here one evening Angus gave one of the most striking demonstrations of his giant strength. Beaching his boat in the fading light, he asked a crowd of idlers on the shore, fellow fishermen all of them, to give him a hand in hauling his big boat up the steep and stony slope. The fishermen accordingly seized the bowline and hauled away, with Angus pushing and guiding the boat from the stern. The fishermen didn't stop at high water mark, however, but to play a prank they kept the boat moving up to the crest of the bank, gleefully hoping to launch it on the other side in the lagoon pond. Seeing what they were up to, Angus caught the stern of the boat in both hands and held on, planting both feet firmly in the deep shingle and setting his massive frame to prevent any further movement of the heavy craft. The boat stopped; the crowd of fishermen set themselves and heaved with renewed vigor; Angus as determinedly held on.

Suddenly there was a wrenching and cracking, and the entire transom, the solid and heavy piece of wood that filled the entire back end of the boat, came away in Angus's hands. The boat had literally been pulled to pieces!

Gille Mor, "The Big Boy," had by now grown into the Cape Breton Giant. At nineteen he was already more than seven feet, two inches high—and still growing more than an inch and a half a year. He weighed more than four hundred pounds, and his arms, from palm to palm outstretched, could span over eleven feet. His tremendous shoulders, the centre of his vast strength, were forty-four inches wide, and his feet were fourteen inches long. He was unbelievably powerful, yet seemed heedless of his fantastic strength. He once carried a 190-pound man, a friend who had become exhausted on a midnight walk through deep snow on the way home from a party, on his back for miles, yet was so engrossed in conversation that he was unaware when his friend slipped off and walked behind. He was so strong that the man's weight on his back was a matter of no significance to him at all. When a nearby merchant jokingly told a St. Ann's customer asking for credit that he could have all the barrels of flour that he or anyone else could throw up from the hold onto the deck of the vessel unloading at his wharf, the quick-thinking customer enlisted the Giant's help. In no time at all Angus had tossed half a dozen heavy barrels of flour from the bottom of the hold onto the deck, and some even into the water alongside—then packed them on his shoulders to the neighbour's waiting cart.

All these feats of strength, all these tales of prowess, inevitably spread the fame of the Cape Breton Giant abroad, and aroused interest in the commercial possibilities of such a prodigy in the world of entertainment. For Angus, the moment of truth came during a visit with some of the Mac-

Leod boys to nearby Neil's Harbour, where he was approached by a Captain Samuel Dunseith, a Yankee schooner skipper and entrepreneur. Captain Dunseith was impressed, not only by the size of the nineteen-year-old giant, but also by his good looks; Angus was a fine-looking young man of good proportions, despite his great size, and with deep blue eyes, curly black hair, pleasant manners and a fine musical voice.

Dunseith offered to put him on the stage, with the American acting as his agent, and painted the usual glowing picture of lots of money and a gentleman's life. It was a difficult offer for Angus to decline, since it came at a time when the little colony of St. Ann's was entering the period of famine and depression that was eventually to force most of its inhabitants to follow their pastor, Norman McLeod, far over the seas to a new home in New Zealand. The MacAskills did not want to part with their son, nor was Angus himself anxious to leave home, but the opportunity to earn desperately-needed money at a time when the whole community was faced with famine was too great an opportunity to be missed; in the early summer of 1849, the Cape Breton Giant went on tour.

The stories of the Giant's stage appearances are often conflicting, and some are palpably untrue; most of the stories concerning his travels are apocryphal and cannot be verified. Certainly the famous photograph still to be seen on ancient posters, showing the famous Barnum midget Tom Thumb sitting on the Giant's outstretched hand, was an elaborate fake. People in St. Ann's believed that the Giant toured with Tom Thumb under the auspices of P.T. Barnum, the great impresario of the times, but it seems that the photograph was made for publicity purposes from two separate negatives. There is no record that the dwarf and the giant ever met, or indeed that the Giant was ever shown by Barnum; it is possible that he appeared briefly at one of Barnum's "museums" in New York or Philadelphia but no evidence has survived.

What is certain is that Angus appeared in Yarmouth, Halifax and other Maritime centres en-route to the United States, and that there he toured extensively. There are posters in the Nova Scotia archives made for his appearances at Mason's Hall in Halifax, where he appeared for two "Levees" daily, performing feats of strength and answering questions from the curious crowd. In July 1849 he toured Quebec and Lower Canada before departing on a lengthy tour of the midwestern States, only then being opened up by the new railroads. Once a train on which he was traveling was boarded by bandits, but the gunmen fled when the Giant stood up from his seat and faced them, his bulk filling the narrow aisle and touching the low roof of the carriage.

Angus was kept close to his hotel room in the towns he visited, since people were unlikely to pay a dollar to see him in a theatre if they could see him for nothing in the street outside. Yet for publicity purposes he made a number of planned appearances in public; one of the more memorable was in a western town where he entered a tavern and called for a drink for all hands. As everyone present raised their glasses, Angus stepped to the bar where an enormous puncheon, reputed to hold

140 gallons of Scotch whiskey, stood in the corner. Angus struck the top with his fist, causing the bung to pop from the barrel, then lifted the huge barrel over his head and, from the open bunghole, drank the health of his admiring audience.

In those days he was splendidly attired in a cutaway coat, complete with the fashionable velvet collar; a waistcoat of white brocade which measured five feet two inches around; fashionably cut trousers and elegant shoes; all topped with a magnificent beaver hat, specially made for him in Paris, which measured 26 1/2 inches around the brim. On some appearances he varied his costume with a dashing uniform, custom tailored for him in the United States.

It is difficult today to trace accurately the extensive tours of the Cape Breton Giant; certainly he toured not only all of North America but through the West Indies and possible South America as well. He traveled in Europe, and appears to have met Queen Victoria herself, although accounts of the occasion differ as to circumstances and place; Windsor Castle is the locale most favoured by surviving accounts. MacAskill tradition says that the Queen presented him with a Highland costume, especially made for him, and in view of Victoria's celebrated predilection for the Highlands and Highlanders, such a gift seems quite in character, and he seems also to have received from her hands two gold rings.

But it was in New Orleans that Big Angus gave his most celebrated, and fateful, display of strength. On the river wharves there the Giant was goaded by the taunts of a handful of French sailors into an attempt to lift a cast-iron anchor which was lying on the shore, and which was later found to weigh 2,700 pounds—nearly a ton and a half! He lifted the enormous weight easily in a neatly-executed "press lift," but somehow in doing so he seems to have caught a fluke of the anchor in his shoulder. It crippled him for a time, and although he later shook off the more obvious effects of the accident, the injury was to plague him for the rest of his days.

Eventually, after years of wandering the great cities of two continents, Angus returned home, a relatively wealthy man, to settle down on the shore of St. Ann's Bay. He found a vastly different community; most of the families he had known in boyhood had gone off to New Zealand with Norman McLeod, or in one or another of the subsequent shiploads which set out in the years following. New settlers had moved in, most of them from the western shore of Scotland or the off-lying islands, but a few too from other parts of Nova Scotia.

Today in Englishtown, just across the modern highway from the site of the old MacAskill homestead [now the Giant MacAskill Museum] are the remains of a rectangular foundation, all that exists of the general store built there over a century ago by the Cape Breton Giant. Here the big man spent his years of retirement, operating a general store and living in large rooms upstairs.

Directly across the bay, near Munro's Point, Angus bought the grist mill, built there originally by John Munro, and it is at these two sites that he established the character which so endeared him to his neighbours, an aura of kindness and good nature which survives to this day. He did not like to grant credit, knowing this to be the cause of the downfall of most retail businesses of that day, yet he could never deny a person in need. As a result, his neighbours took ceaseless advantage of his generosity, so that when he died he had uncollected credits outstanding on his books of more than eight hundred pounds sterling; a very large sum for those days.

The shop was a remarkable backdrop for its even more remarkable proprietor. The doorway was nine feet high, and Angus was usually to be found inside, puffing on his pipe, sitting on a stool made from a 140-gallon molasses puncheon. He dispensed tea by the pound scoop or the fistful, whichever the customer preferred; the fistful was by far the better bargain! At his grist mill, his strength was often on display; he picked up four-bushel bags of grain in one hand, and turned over the cumbrous millwheels like so many cookies; millwheels which can still be seen today on the lawn of a Baddeck restaurant. [The millstones are still there. The Thistledown Restaurant is gone, and the property is now part of the Telegraph House.] He was now in the full prime of life, seven feet nine inches tall and a trim 430 pounds in weight. An affable, much-traveled man, he was content to settle down to the life of a prosperous trader and merchant in the community where he had grown up, and where he was established as a popular and respected figure.

Yet few giants live long lives. Angus's father was to survive to the amazing age of 98 and his mother lived to be 80, but for the great Giant the end came with sudden swiftness in his 39th year. Struck down suddenly by what the local doctor diagnosed as "brain fever," whatever that might have been, Angus was assisted from his shop quarters across the road to his parents' house, his boyhood home, and put to bed in his old bedstead, now much too short, which was set up downstairs in the living room. Here, on August 8, 1863, he died in the midst of his family, and in the simple frame house above the bay which, in all his wanderings, he had always considered "home."

The funeral of Cape Breton's Giant was on a scale proportionate to his size. Two carpenters laboured to build a coffin the like of which had never been seen before; contemporary newspaper accounts gloated unctuously over the somber splendour of its fittings and its lining—"white fabric of the finest quality." Yet the casket itself was not an inch larger than it had to be: length, eight feet; breadth, two feet six inches; height, one foot three inches. The funeral ceremony was conducted by the Reverend Abraham MacIntosh, minister of the local Presbyterian church, who had been present at the bedside when Angus died, and who was himself eventually to be laid to rest in a plot next to the Giant's. Burial was in the lovely little cemetery looking out over the Bay St. Ann's which Angus had loved so well and where, in a plot twelve feet long, the Cape Breton Giant was brought to his final resting place by a throng of friends and relatives, and a respectful crowd, old and young, assembled from all over the island.

Today, the Giant's grave, the outline of its mound as impressive in its proportions as those of its occupant, is visited each summer by hundreds of tourists and curious visitors of every sort. Yet its solid tombstone, earnestly read and photographed by so many summer visitors, enshrines a curious error and includes an epitaph vastly different from that originally placed over the Giant's grave. The day of death shown on the stone is given as August 6 instead of the true date, August 8, and the inscription on the modern stone reads: "A dutiful son, a loving brother, a true friend, a loyal subject, a humble Christian."

The original stone, which can be seen today in the Giant's museum, gives the day of death correctly and bears the inscription: "A dutiful son, a kind brother, just in all his dealings. Universally respected by his acquaintance. Mark the perfect man, and behold the upright, for the end of that man is peace."

The discrepancy came about early in the twentieth century, when the Giant's grave was found to be virtually unmarked after more than half a century of neglect. The provincial government arranged for a new stone to be set up, and its data was reconstructed from the memory of surviving friends and relatives, the original stone having disappeared. When the new stone was put in place, however, the old stone was discovered just beneath the surface of the ground, where it had fallen flat and been covered over. It was rescued by Norman Bethune and later presented by him to the museum.

Mementos of the Cape Breton Giant survive today in many parts of both Canada and the United States; his posters are in the provincial archives and one of his enormous uniform dress boots is a popular display in the Citadel museum at Halifax. But it is here, on the shores of the bay where he lived most of his life that his memory best survives; his bed, chair and cane, his great waistcoat, tail-coat and tophat; his life-size photos and other memorabilia fill the museum [at Englishtown], and his graveside is visited by an endless stream of visitors. His name lives in countless relatives, his fame in a hundred stories; his ambiance envelopes the community. The mouldering remains of his house and his store, of his two grist mills now sleep in sunlit serenity ashore near the remains of their mighty owner, but it is the sparkling waters of the bay he loved so well that still are haunted by the spirit of the gentle Giant.

◆ 7 ◆

The Iron Men

Shipbuilding and Seafaring

ON THE SOUTHERN SHORE of the South Gut, or South Haven as it is now called, stands the old pier of St. Ann's. On pilings reaching high out of the water, and driven deep into the seabed beneath, it runs out from the shore in an "L" shape, with a small red-shingled storage shed on it, now piled high with lobster traps. With fourteen feet of water alongside its northern face, and stout bollards for securing lines, it can still provide secure berthing for good-sized vessels, although it is now used only by a few local fishermen as a convenient berth for small inshore boats. [The pier and shed are gone today. See the photograph of how it looked in James Lamb's day, between pages 18 and 19.]

It is a picturesque place, much painted and sketched by visiting artists, with its magnificent backdrop of headland and sea and wooded mountainside. Its weathered timbers are visited only by the occasional angler, or strollers pausing to admire the panorama it affords, particularly of summer sunsets, yet this aging relic, now dreaming its last years away in such solitude, is the last visible link with the great Age of Sail; ships from across the sea once berthed here, and at an earlier wharf a few hundred yards to the east, to discharge or load cargo. Nor was it only visiting ships which this great bay once sheltered; St. Ann's was famous more than a century ago for the ships launched here, and sent its vessels, built on these shores from native woods cut on these hillsides, far across the oceans to foreign lands in every quarter of the globe.

The beginnings of navigation here are lost in the mists of time. Fishermen from Brittany, from Portugal, from the western shores of England and Ireland called here long before Columbus sailed, putting in on voyages to the Banks to repair storm damage in the landlocked shelter of the Bay, or to split and dry their catch ashore, as they did in similar anchorages in nearby Newfoundland. Fishermen of the late Middle Ages were illiterate and left no written record of their voyages, but there is no question that they were regular visitors to the New World before Columbus officially put it on the maps of the European world. There is a record in French archives of a catch being landed from America in 1497, just after Columbus' return, and its phrasing leaves no doubt but that the trade was already a long-established one. European fishermen found that the Mi'kmaq Indians of Cape Breton were already sailors of a sort, equipping their larger canoes, from eighteen to twenty-four feet, with a single square sail of bark or hide in order to take advantage of the winds in sheltered water.

There is a tradition, still recalled by older residents of the area, of a Portuguese presence in St. Ann's Bay; Ingonish, to the north, takes its name from Niganiche, the name given by Portuguese fishermen to the little fort they built there. Nearby Sydney was originally called Baie des Espagnols or Spanish Bay; the name survives on Admiralty charts to this day. But it was principally French ships which seem to have made this bay their base; French fishermen who dried their catches on its shores, French men-o'-war which lay snug behind the guns of Fort Dauphin, and French trading ships which arrived heavily-laden with supplies for New France and departed with bales of furs and scurvy-wracked invalids for the long voyage home to Le Havre or St. Malo. The French built ships here on the sloping foreshore west of Fort Dauphin; mostly small vessels for coastwise trade, but also a powerful frigate, and cannonballs from their warships are still found occasionally by fishermen on the sandy bottom of the bay where French fleets anchored hundreds of years before.

With the departure of the French after the fall of Louisbourg, the bay was used only by occasional fishermen until the coming of the *Ark* with Norman McLeod and his Scottish followers opened a new era of shipping activity. From the beginning, all trade and communication between the new Highland community and its neighbours at Pictou, Sydney or Baddeck was by sea; the wilderness ashore was virtually impenetrable save for a few paths linking individual farms with one another. This situation was to prevail right up to the coming of the railroad in the late 1890s, which provided the first land communication with the outside world, and the roadbuilding of the twentieth century, which for the first time allowed the individual Cape Bretoner to move about his island with some degree of freedom without recourse to the sea. Before that, it was always easier to travel twenty miles by sea—or on the ice, in winter—than one mile overland.

The Scottish settlers who followed the Reverend Norman McLeod to St. Ann's were as much fishermen as farmers, accustomed to the sea and its ways from earliest times in their original Hebridean homes. They were also skilled from boyhood in the use of the rough carpentry tools of the day; the broadaxe, the ripsaw, the adze, the mallet. From the beginning, the little Scottish settlement at St. Ann's was busy with boats built by individual families for use in fishing along the shore, or for communication back and forth across the bay. The shores of North and South Guts were lined with them, but most of the traffic in seagoing cargo and passengers was borne in ships built elsewhere, and berthing at the rough jetties on the north side of North Gut, at Black Cove, and on the southern shore of South Gut, which provided the deepest and most accessible berths of all.

After a few years, however, the tough farmer-fishermen began to combine their labours, particularly in the off-season months of early winter and spring when weather kept them from other work about their homesteads, to build vessels of larger size to serve their manifold needs. Shallops—bluff-bowed, square-sterned two-masted gaff-riggers—and schooners and pinkies—high-sterned double-enders—were built to carry small cargoes along the coast, most of these little vessels being under sixty feet long. They were built anywhere along the shore where there was sufficient water close offshore to float the finished craft, and sufficient timber on the hillside nearby with which to construct her. Keels, stems and sternposts were of oak, if available; floors of elm or some other good hardwood, frames of juniper and beams of planking of good spruce.

Gangs of men dragged tree trunks from the nearby woods to deep sawpits where two men, one in the pit, the other above, sawed the trunks into planks. When one considers that such planks might be twenty feet or more in length, the labour of sawing them from huge tree trunks can be imagined, but it is unlikely that anyone today can conceive of the agony of discomfort entailed in standing in a hot, dark clay pit, with sawdust pouring down on one's upturned face, and shoving upwards with all one's strength at the handle of a vast saw. To our effete age, the hardihood of the pioneer is beyond belief.

The timbers were adzed to fit the lines followed by eye, assisted by a little half-model carved from wood, from which the curves and angles and measurements could be calculated. Frames were set up and attached to the keel, laid out on raised keelblocks on the chosen site, by long iron bolts called treenails. Planking was spiked to the frames, the hull decked in; masts were usually stepped after launching. The whole operation, from the forging of the ironwork to the cutting of the virgin forest, was carried out on the spot, with the single exception of the rigging. Canvas sails and hempen rigging had always to be purchased from European sources, the only items which the enterprising shipbuilders of St. Ann's could not provide themselves.

In 1845 a ship was launched which was to

open a new era in the life of St. Ann's, and appropriately, it was launched by John Munro, far and away the most enterprising man in the community. His new yard at Shipyard Point was ideally located for the construction of sailing ships, with a long, sloping foreshore and easy access to the best stands of timber all along the north shores of the bay. Here, in the summer of 1845, he launched the first ship; that is, a vessel of three masts carrying square sail on each mast. She was a magnificent ship for her time and place; christened the *Chieftain*, she had as figurehead a fine woodcarving of a man in full Highland dress. Measuring 440 tons, she was infinitely bigger than anything seen at St. Ann's since the days of the French frigates, and she represented the first commercial undertaking in the local shipbuilding field, having been built, from the first, to be sold abroad for deep-sea voyaging.

Her launch was accompanied by much ceremony, with pipers playing bravely ashore and bunting flying from the ship afloat, but her departure for overseas was even more of an event. The shores were lined with people come to see the ship sail away to a new life on the trackless seas beyond their bay, and it marked a turning point in the lives of many, particularly the young men. Eyes and thoughts began to turn outward, from the limited life of the close-knit colony to the endless possibilities that lay just over the horizon. It was a crew of such young men that sailed the *Chieftain* to England and, eventually, to her port of registry at Galway in Ireland. Increasingly, the young men of St. Ann's turned to ocean voyaging as a way of life; in the peak years of the Age of Sail during the last half of the nineteenth century, thousands of Cape Bretoners sailed the oceans and seas of the world in ships wearing the flags of all the maritime nations, and in St. Ann's, the sea became a way of life.

Not even the sons of the Reverend Norman McLeod himself were immune; all of them succumbed to the restlessness of the sea and young Donald, who sailed away originally in the schooner *Maria*, a small vessel built nearby at Big Bras d'Or, ended that voyage in the United Kingdom, a confirmed sailor. It was his subsequent series of voyages, which culminated in Australia, which was eventually to lead his redoubtable father and his flock from St. Ann's all the way to the remote Antipodes.

But the *Chieftain* was responsible for a dramatic change in the fortunes of the older people also in the little community where she was built. For her great commercial success—she was reputed to have made John Munro a rich man overnight—prompted imitation, and from this date St. Ann's became a centre of the shipbuilding industry. The wooden ships of Nova Scotia, and the iron men who sailed them, were to become famous the world over, and founded a legend which survives to this day. There is hardly a home along the shores of the great bay which does not have its associations with the sea; with an ancestor who built ships on the shoreline, or who sailed in them to far distant places.

At Shipyard Point, near Munro's Point on the north shore of St. Ann's Bay—the chief centre of shipbuilding operations during the great era of sail—the atmosphere of those days can still be vividly recalled. The point, a long, narrow spit of low-lying, wooded land, culminating in a sheltering hook of boulders, is reached today by a narrow, overgrown path which follows the route of the original road by which supplies were once hauled to the busy yards. Now a mere track, the road is still clearly evident, and much of the growth which now encumbers it is of fairly recent date. At the outer end of the point, a low shore runs evenly into deep water; old residents of the area recall the launching ways still reaching out into the harbour from the shore, and part of one of these, a massive length of lumber made from a squared log, still lies on the foreshore [in the 1970s]. A curving spit of boulders makes an ideal breakwater for the launching site, giving shelter from the easterly winds blowing in off the sea, and from the swell which would be the principal hazard. On the low shore behind can still be made out the rectangular pits which are the remains of foundations, marking the sites of various building and storage sheds, and the piles of stone which are the remains of a chimney. The blacksmith shop, with its three distinct forges, can still be clearly seen, together with the roads and ramps by which material was hauled and assembled. Everywhere there is evidence of energy and bustle and business; an atmosphere which contrasts markedly with the silence and darkness of the forest which has engulfed this once-thriving industry. All about are enormous pieces of rotting timber, of rusting iron; below a thin blanket of moss and leaves lie the bones of this old shipyard, like the skeleton of some great beast of the past.

The most dramatic survival is the great anchor stone; a huge rectangular boulder of granite, over ten feet high and roughly fifteen feet square, which looms through the surrounding saplings like a mastodon at bay. In the eery light of the thick woods, its sudden bulk is almost frightening; there is nothing like it to be found anywhere in the area.

This tremendous piece of heavy stone still bears the marks of its use by seamen and shipbuilders over the centuries. For the French used it, three hundred years ago, according to legend, and possibly the Breton fishermen ages before that. The corners are bitten deep and its sides scored by the cables and chains which have been fastened around it, for located on the low land so close to the sheltered anchorage, it has always provided an ideal mooring point for a vessel securing to the shore. But it was chiefly used during the shipbuilding era, as a permanent anchoring point for the cables by which ships winched themselves up or down the sloping ways; for launching new ships or hauling out old ones for repair.

All about the base of this great rock are a series of shallow pits, the legacy of treasure-seekers. For legend has it that a wealthy Acadian family, forced to move elsewhere when these French-speaking settlers refused to take an oath of allegiance to the British crown, buried the family wealth here, at this enduring, unique and easily-found landmark. “A barrel of gold,” is how the locals tell it, and still diggers come to poke hopefully about the great rock. Only a few remnants of rusty iron have rewarded their efforts so far, but always, there is hope. Anchor Rock on Shipyard Point is the Oak Island of St. Ann’s Bay, but it is its many relics from the great age of shipbuilding which are its true treasure.

In 1846, a year after the *Chieftain*'s successful voyage, John MacLeod launched a large brig, the *Norman*, named after the renowned pastor of St. Ann's. Of 247 tons burthen, she was completed for an owner in nearby Sydney Mines, T.D. Archibald, who used her for a year to carry coal to the mainland from the newly-opened mines in the area. The following year, with the rise in ship prices brought about by the developing trade between industrialized Britain and the rest of the world, he sailed her to the United Kingdom and sold her to London owners at a handsome profit.

Her new owner kept the ship's original name and her dour figurehead, a carved likeness of the Reverend Norman McLeod, whom Mr. Archibald had met and greatly admired.

Then began the construction in St. Ann's of a long succession of vessels, great and small, the larger ones nearly always being built for overseas trading to a Britain hungry for raw materials to feed her burgeoning factories, while the smaller went into coastal trading during the summer months, and south to the West Indies in the winter. Dried cod from the Banks was one of the few foods which kept well in the hot Caribbean before the days of refrigeration, and was a staple of the diet of the Negro plantation workers in the West Indian islands. Most of the little brigs and schooners which plied there from Nova Scotia returned with their holds filled with hogsheads of molasses and rum. Rum thus became far and away the cheapest and most plentiful spirit available on the

Atlantic seaboard, and its effect on the drinking habits of Maritimers, and particularly Cape Bretoners, survives to this day. A glass of rum is to the St. Ann's Scot today what a dram of whiskey was to his Highland forebears long before: the traditional standard of hospitality.

One of the most notable vessels built in St. Ann's was the barque *Flora*, built by John Munro and launched at his now-famous yard in 1847. For that time she was enormous and her building and fitting out strained the resources of the little community of artisan-farmers. The largest ship built in Cape Breton at that time, she was of 725 tons burthen, and of handsome proportions, boasting a fine figurehead of a female figure to represent her namesake. She had been built to John Munro's own account, but was sold on launching to new owners in Halifax and never returned to her native bay.

Another well-known vessel built in St. Ann's was the brig, *Richard Brown*, launched here also in 1847. She was built for a triumvirate of owners, the Young brothers, Walter and John, and Richard Laffin, and was named after the celebrated manager of the General Mining Association. A great load-carrier, this full-lined brig was later sold to J.B. Ward of Newfoundland, and made a voyage which was described vividly in contemporary newspapers. While on voyage from Sydney to Halifax she encountered such bad weather that she was blown all the way south to the Caribbean, eventually making port in the island of St. Thomas in the Virgins. After making good her considerable storm damage, she set out again for Halifax, where she eventually arrived after an interval of more than two months and after covering thousands of miles of ocean on what should have been a short passage. This famous vessel had a long and busy life, being sold to Irish owners and still being on the shipping register in the 1870's.

The same T.D. Archibald who had been the owner of the successful *Flora* also commissioned the *Christina*, of 98 tons, built by Angus Mullen at St. Ann's and launched in 1849, but this prominent shipowner was by now involved in the financing of a much more notable vessel. This was the *Margaret*, now underway at Black Cove, the famous ship which was to carry the Reverend Norman McLeod and his followers around the world to Australia. Mr. Archibald advanced two hundred pounds sterling as a loan against a substantial interest in the vessel, which he later recovered when she was successfully sold in Australia. Rigged as a barque, with square canvas on fore and main and fore-and-aft sails only on the mizzen, the *Margaret* was of 246 tons burthen. She was assembled on stocks at Black Cove, and most of the timber for her construction was cut nearby from woods on the McLeod property. A fine model of her is on display today at the Gaelic College.

With her sailing in October 1851, with 140 St. Ann's residents aboard, much of the heart went out of the community, but shipbuilding and seafaring continued as the way of life of the Scots who remained at St. Ann's, and those who arrived over later years to settle here.

In 1850 Angus MacLeod built a schooner, the *Emily G. Corbett*, to his own account, and sailed her in the Newfoundland and coastal trade for many years. He died aboard her and was buried at sea.

In 1851, the year of the *Margaret*'s departure, a handsome brigantine, the *Paragon*, was launched at St. Ann's by Angus MacMillan. She, too, was bought by T.D. Archibald and ran for a time in the coal trade before being sold to Newfoundland owners in 1853. A handy vessel of 155 tons, she enjoyed a long life, being operated by Alex Gordon of Dublin, Ireland, nearly thirty years after her launch. In view of the nature of her heavy cargoes, and the weather of the North Atlantic in which she did all her voyaging, her long life, and that of so many of her contemporaries, speaks volumes for the quality of work and materials put into ships built at St. Ann's.

In 1851 John Munro launched at his shipyard a new style of vessel: a big brigantine, the *Victor*, with a round stern, a marked departure from the flat transom and pinky double-enders which were the normal designs of earlier years. A fine vessel of 126 tons, she went to new owners in Halifax upon completion.

A remarkable vessel, launched in 1853, was the big barque *George Hughes*, built in St. Ann's by Angus MacMillan whose *Paragon* had been such a success. Of 253 tons, the *Hughes* was described in contemporary newspaper accounts as being "a very fine vessel, built of the best materials available." Owned by George Lewis of North Sydney, she was towed to that port on completion by the steamer *Banshee*, making the passage in the smart time of five hours. She was later sold to interests in the United States. John Munro eventually followed his old leader to New Zealand, and his shipyard on the little point fell silent, but other ships continued to pour out from other yards around the shores of St. Ann's. There was the *Quickstep* in 1856 for William Ross, the *Vernant* in 1860 for Kenneth Morrison, the *Enoch Benner* in 1861 for the MacIvors, George and Archibald; the *Greyhound* in 1863 for Angus and Donald MacRitchie. The following year there was the brigantine *Chilo* of 207 tons, for Halifax owners, and a remarkably fine brig, the *Quango*, of 145 tons, was built here by Robert Kerr for J.A. Butler of Halifax. She was notable for a round stern and a superb figurehead, carved on the spot by an artist whose name has not survived.

The last big sailing vessel built at St. Ann's was the *Lady Aberdeen* of 88 tons, launched by Alex Gunn in 1894. After a notable career, including a stranding at Gabarus, she passed to Prince Edward Island owners, and was eventually wrecked off Savage Harbour in that island at the turn of the century.

By this time the age of sail, and the glory of the Nova Scotia ships and men, had passed its zenith. Steel ships were beyond the technology of the little community at St. Ann's, and steamships had supplanted wind-driven ships on all the major ocean routes. Sail hung on the fishing and coastal trades, but mostly the ships calling in at the wharf at St. Ann's were steam powered, and after the coming of the railway in the late 1890's traffic up to the little wharf in South Gut dwindled with each passing year.

The maritime tradition lived on—and lives on—at St. Ann's, but today the boats that use the bay are the small powerboats of inshore fishermen, and the ferry carrying cars back and forth from Englishtown to Jersey Cove Beach. The pilings and timbers of piers and shipyards have long since rotted away; only the little wharf at South Haven stands to mark the passing of an age. The lobstermen and car ferry plying the bay today are the inheritors of a Maritime tradition that stretches back through the barques and brigs and full-rigged ships of the great age and the frigates of the Sun King to the warships of Daniel, and even beyond to the tough lugsailed shallops of medieval fishermen. For this forest-ringed bay has always been a port of note, and its wooden ships and iron men have voyaged from here to the farthest seas, the remotest harbours. The waters that lap about the pilings in this forgotten corner of South Gut stretch unbroken to the Antipodes and the Sulu Sea, linking its spruce and granite to the palms and coral on the other side of the world.

• 8 •

The Legacy

The Gaelic College at St. Ann's

AFTER THE *MARGARET* SAILED from St. Ann's in 1851, the depopulation of Norman's old colony continued; as the migrants became more established in New Zealand, so their letters to those at home in St. Ann's became ever more encouraging, and over the next few years the steady attrition continued. By 1860 the densely-settled Highland community which Norman had built up around his little peninsula between the two guts was only a memory, and already a new pattern of settlement was taking shape. On Norman's land, John Robertson had established his family in Norman's old home, and here too he boarded the first Presbyterian minister to replace Norman at the Big Church on a permanent basis, the Reverend Abraham MacIntosh, a graduate, ironically enough, of the Boularderie Academy which Norman had so detested.

But the old days were gone forever; now the parishioners were drawn from a much more widely-spread and thinly-populated area, scattered at little farmsteads strung along the new and growing network of primitive roadways. The old church was no longer so convenient as it had been, standing in splendid isolation above Black Cove. A new congregation was split off, building St. Mark's on the old Indian campsite in Englishtown. Finally, in 1894, a new building was located at the head of South Gut, more convenient to parishioners along the south shore. It was built intentionally to the same overall dimensions as the Big Church at Black Cove, although without the gallery and with less seating, and as the old building grew derelict, this became the base for the congregation of St. Ann's. Today it is called Ephraim Scott Memorial Church, standing at the roadside of Highway 105 just west of the causeway junction with the Cabot Trail [at South Haven], but it perpetuates still both the shell of its vanished predecessor and the congregation founded by the Reverend Norman McLeod.

On the little peninsula which was once the centre of the Norman empire, things went from bad to worse. John Robertson, finding the old McLeod homestead too confining, had built himself a grand new residence a hundred yards away. A gracious and beautifully-built house, called "The Red House" because of its deep ochre stain, it was a landmark for more than a century, being finally pulled down in 1973; its solid foundations, of big stones, worked and squared, still dominate the property today. But despite this gesture, the fortunes of the Robertson estate went steadily downhill; when he died, and his hundreds of acres were disposed of according to the instructions of his will, the total sum realized was a mere pittance, land values having shrunk to virtually nothing. His widow and second wife was left with little money to keep up the house, other than the board paid by a brother, and she died virtually a pauper. With her passing, the Red House and the property about it began a long period of varying fortunes, of changing ownership, of increasing disuse and misuse, neglect and decline.

There is a corner of this land which is still virtually unknown today, even among old-established residents. If one follows the old road down to Black Cove, now mostly overgrown by spruce bush, the remains of an old footpath can still be made out branching off toward the western part of the cove. Threading among the trees and marshy patches, the forgotten trail leads to a low promontory jutting out into the water, thickly overgrown with trees. In the heart of this little grove is a square stone wall, of more than waist height, without gate or opening of any kind. It looks rather like a miniature fort, its massive walls still unbroken despite the ravages of a large birch tree which has thrust its trunk up through it. There appears to be nothing inside, apart from a clump of birch, but just outside is a small tumulus marked by little stones at head and foot, which is obviously a grave of some sort.

This curious structure, now almost completely swallowed up by the wilderness and forgotten by the community, represents the last resting place of John Robertson, whose money made possible the McLeod emigration to Australia and who lived like a laird at the Red House at the centre of the Reverend Norman's old empire. He lies buried here in state, with a wife on either side of him; the wall was put up by his widow about the graves of her husband and his first wife, and she joined him there years later. It is said that the wall was put up by a mason from Baddeck as repayment for room and board at the impoverished Red House, and after more than a century of neglect it is still impressive. If there were ever headstones inside the enclosure, they have long since vanished.

The grave outside is apparently that of an infant, said to be the child of an unmarried servant girl. The breath of ancient scandal still invests this lonely place, the details long forgotten; the tiny grave, ostracized for eternity from its sanctified elders outside the forbidding wall of enduring stone, has enshrined for all time the values and attitudes of a proud society in a harsh age, certain of its Christian rectitude.

With the passing of the Robertsons, the links between the increasingly fragmented community of St. Ann's and their forebears grew ever more tenuous. With the establishment of new congregations at Englishtown and South Haven, the old church at Black Cove, once the dynamic centre of a close-knit community, disappeared entirely, its last timbers borne away to build barns and houses. The slipways at Shipyard Point, the schoolhouse of Alexander Munro at Boularderie, the grist mills and buildings of the Norman era, all gradually disappeared, leaving only a memory in the collective consciousness of a generation now grown old.

New roads replaced old; new groupings—municipal, educational, religious, social, administrative—forged new loyalties. Where once had been St. Ann's, a viable, close-knit community, there grew to be in the twentieth century a host of new social identities: Englishtown, South Haven, North Gut, North River, and many more. The past, even so vivid and colourful a past as that of St. Ann's, was in danger of being totally submerged in the ubiquitous banality of the present, and with it the roots and traditions which confer strength and identity in an increasingly faceless world.

All this was changed by one man, and by one man alone: a Presbyterian minister named Angus W.R. MacKenzie.

This remarkable man, in many ways a latter-day incarnation of the Reverend Norman McLeod, was born in 1891 at Portree, the lovely little port town on the Isle of Skye, and after serving in the Black Watch in World War I he arrived at Baddeck as minister to the Presbyterian congregation, in the middle of the depression years preceding World War II. As a Scot and a clergyman he was familiar with the story of the Reverend Norman McLeod, and soon became fascinated by the innumerable sites and associations linking St. Ann's with this towering figure from the romantic past. Interest quickened into concern; concern to crusade; crusade to obsession; this determined and dynamic man literally devoted the rest of his days to restoring the Highland tradition in Cape Breton, and to reawakening in its people a consciousness of the priceless legacy bequeathed them by their pioneer forebears.

In many ways, not all of them unconscious, this remarkable man came increasingly to resemble the hero he set out to immortalize. Like the Reverend Norman, "A.W.R."—as he came to be known—was a man of forceful and even dominating personality; able, energetic, and blessed with remarkable power of intellect and character. Like him, he possessed in high degree the ability to concentrate his energies on an ultimate objective to the exclusion of all else, and to bring to bear all the power of his exceptional personality upon each successive step toward its attainment. Like him, too, he was autocratic, overbearing, often difficult; a man who aroused strong feelings, one way or another, in all who knew him.

His objective was to restore the pride of the Highland families of Cape Breton in their proud heritage, not only in their Scottish roots in the old world, but in their pioneering achievements in the new. His plan was two-fold; to establish a museum enshrining the Scottish-Canadian achievements of the past, and to found a centre which would perpetuate the Highland traditions in the future.

It would be difficult to exaggerate the extent of his achievement; indeed, given the impoverished condition of the region in relation to the rest of North America, and the depressed nature of the economy of the entire world, beyond anything in human experience, his success seems incredible. For not only did he found a college, set up a museum, restore a people's pride in their Highland tradition, but he also reshaped a region, helped found its greatest industry, and instituted changes which affect the lives of every man, woman and child living in Cape Breton today. In terms of magnitude of effect, it was an achievement that eclipsed even that of the illustrious predecessor whose fame he set out to perpetuate.

Early in his crusade, MacKenzie set his heart on acquiring the property which had been the centre both of Norman McLeod's personal holdings and of the church and community which he headed: the lovely peninsula at the head of St. Ann's Bay, between North and South Guts. To provide a proper focus for the historical associations of the area, he determined to establish a museum there to its pioneers, and in order to perpetuate the distinctive Highland culture, he decided to also locate there an establishment to teach the arts of piping, dancing and handcrafts associated with it, as well as Gaelic, the ancient language of the Scots. The Gaelic College which today embodies these functions is the singular achievement of a singular man.

It stands today in the place where A.W.R. wished it to be: crowning the high point of land overlooking the McLeod peninsula, and commanding magnificent views of the entire bay and the sea beyond. The [original] buildings which were set about the central lawns were built of logs, in deference to pioneer methods of construction, and were of modest, even austere appearance in keeping with the Highland traditions they enshrined. Their simplicity set off the breathtaking magnificence of their surroundings; the view from the open-air amphitheatre on its hillside can hardly be surpassed anywhere. A museum houses not only artifacts of the pioneer era of the region, but a range of memorabilia of Giant MacAskill, and others associated with Norman McLeod, including an unusual number of mementos from the McLeod colony in New Zealand. The wide range of handcrafts produced on the premises include tartans woven on the college's hand looms, and these and other products of Highland crafts are sold in the college's own shop.

This unique institution represents A.W.R.'s

dream come true; here, in these simple dormitories and classrooms, come students from all over North America, and even beyond; young men and women who make up the student body for the summer semesters. Here they master the Highland arts of weaving and piping, of dancing and drumming. Here the ancient language of the Gaels is taught to young people a world away from the blue hills of Scotland, who live in the urban jungles of Cleveland or Los Angeles or Toronto. Here on this beautiful hilltop ancient Scotland lives anew, just as A.W.R. had hoped it would, a living dream come true, and all about it is the evidence of A.W.R.'s hand.

There is the old McLeod property to begin with, the little point with all its associations with the memorable past. In the heart of the greatest economic depression ever known, A.W.R. had persuaded its owner to part with it; had talked wealthy men into large donations, people of modest means into small ones; had wheedled a grant from this government minister, a tax concession from that municipality. Above all, he had enlisted the support of hundreds of local men and women, whetting their enthusiasm for a community endeavour which dwarfed anything known before in the province, and after a series of meetings in the late 1930s he saw the college founded and on its way just before World War Two intervened.

Once established, the college flourished; today its summer seminars are crowded with students, its annual Mod the highlight of a province-wide series of Highland games sparked by the Gaelic revival, and its concerts in the open-air amphitheatre are the most popular events of the year in the area.

Founding the college was only part of A.W.R.'s achievement; the land itself was shaped and altered to suit his dream. The causeway across which the highway approaches the college crosses the shallow head of South Gut, then climbs the hill in a series of easy curves, cut through thick forest by government engineers at A.W.R.'s urging. The old road it replaced can still be seen, turning off the modern highway at the Ephraim Scott Memorial Church. It meanders across the river that runs into South Gut, and then peters out in farmland on the hillside beyond. Its course can still be followed, however, and the pilings which carried it across the head of South Gut can be seen in the shallow water west of the causeway as one crosses on the modern road and approaches the college hill. This new route was incorporated into the modern scenic drive now famous as the Cabot Trail, and the college itself is not the least of this renowned road's tourist attractions, just as A.W.R. MacKenzie had predicted. The college, the causeway, the scenic trail, the tourist trade; all these, the creations of so many people and today so fundamental a part of Cape Breton life, owe their inspiration to the tireless drive of one restless, energetic, autocratic man.

He had left the church, eventually; he had for many years sadly neglected his ministry, first at Baddeck and later at South Haven, in order to pursue his dream and, as he saw it, his greater charge. In 1947 he became the full-time director of the Gaelic College and resigned entirely from the ministry. All his efforts and energies were now directed toward his dream of a revitalized Highland legacy, and when he died twenty years later the dream was an established reality.

By a supreme irony, he lies today where it is most fitting that he should, contrary to the stipulations of his own will. For he had charged his executors to lay his remains in the quiet churchyard at Spencerville, in far-off Ontario, where he had conducted his first ministry. He died a widower, and virtually penniless; all the money he had raised had been spent, like his own energies, on the attainment of his dream, and at the end there was nothing left over. He died in 1967 on the Saturday of the May 24th holiday weekend; his will, locked in a bank vault, could not be read until the following Tuesday. Wisely, his two sisters decided to bury A.W.R. where he had lived his most meaningful years, and in sight of his most singular accomplishment. It was not until after the funeral that his will revealed Spencerville as his designated resting place, and then it was too late. His simple bronze headstone was embossed with a thistle, his name, and the years of his birth and death; nothing more. His true memorial lies all about him.

He lies today in South Haven cemetery on the shores of lovely St. Ann's Bay, looking out towards the Reverend Norman McLeod's old Scottish colony, and the college he himself had founded to perpetuate its Highland traditions. And the visitor to the quiet graveyard, reflecting on the careers of these two Scottish clergymen, so similar in so many ways, may well ponder on whose was the greater accomplishment, which the greater man.

◆ 9 ◆

L'Envoi

I WALK, on a still summer evening, down the rutted laneway behind the Gaelic College, once the roadway to Norman McLeod's little kingdom, and stand on the grassy hillside near the ruins of his house. It is quiet here, and the fading sunlight invests this storied place, haunted by the ghosts of so many dramas, all long past, with a quality of timelessness that stirs one's imagination; it is a place of dreams.

From far above and behind, comes the distant sound of pipes; some solitary student is working on a march. Faint but without falter it comes to us: "All the Blue Bonnets Are Over the Border."

Across the waters of the bay, now glowing pink in the sunset, Fort Dauphin lies below its grassy mounds, its dream of empire lost forever, and scattered in unmarked graves beneath its sod sleep the nameless Frenchmen, scores of them, who died in pursuit of those dreams. Champlain was here, and the fleets of the Sun King himself [Louis XIV of France] once lay at anchor in these waters. All that now remains is a fading legend, a few plans and documents in dusty archives.

On every side, the past whispers to us: those tumbled stones mark the house of a man who followed a restless star across endless seas and oceans, whose vision inspired hundreds of men and women to follow him in a common destiny to the remote places of the earth. There, in that silent cove, they built their ship; and there, beside the shore, a low mound traces the outline of the great church they put up, once the most celebrated building in the land. Across that narrow stretch of water, by that long spit of boulders, ships were launched that sailed to the great ports of Europe and beyond; at that deserted wharf, mirrored on the waters of South Haven, merchantmen from the West Indies once berthed, their dark-skinned crews in straw hats singing outlandish shanties, their holds redolent of rum and molasses.

JUST ACROSS THE SOUTH GUT from where we stand, the Gentle Giant lived out his brief span; for all his size and strength his grave there in the little cemetery by the bay is as silent as the rest of them.

Behind us, the setting sun flares in a last moment of glory, turning the waters of the bay before us into a breathtaking pool of lambent glory. Around us the hills and headlands gather about them their evening mantle of mist; it is a prospect beautiful beyond words. The piper behind salutes the dying day with a final march; even here we can make out "Scotland the Brave."

Standing here, in this place at this moment, it is impossible not to be deeply moved. Yet it is not the beauty of time or place, the piper's tune nor the pathos of romantic fancy which strikes so deeply to the very centre of our being.

It is its associations, rather than the place itself, which stab to the heart. For I am a Canadian, and all about me is the story of my country.

A Walking Tour

of the Reverend Norman McLeod Settlement at the Gaelic College in St. Ann's—Today

ON THE GROUNDS of the Gaelic College, you can take a lovely, easy walk to the remnants of the Reverend Norman McLeod settlement overlooking Black Cove and St. Ann's Bay.

Ask at the Gaelic College office, or at the St. Ann's Bay-Waipu Twinning Society office at the Gaelic College, and they'll tell you where the well-kept road begins. But you can find it easily on your own. It's at the right-hand side of the property when you face the Gaelic College with your back toward the Cabot Trail. Your first stop is the site of Reverend Norman McLeod's house. As you stroll the road, watch on your left for a gnarled apple tree. It's up on the knoll, not far from the road. At the foot of the tree, you'll see the obvious basement and foundation stones of Norman McLeod's home. Imagine when all those fields were cleared, and the view went out across all of St. Ann's Bay.

Now, return to the road and continue on a short distance. On your right you'll notice foundation stones of an old barn, probably the barn for the John Robertson property. John Robertson bought the land when Norman McLeod left in 1851. A little further along, and in the field on your left you'll find the foundation of the Red House—John Robertson's home. You can still see the shape of the main part of the house, where the chimney once stood, and the entrance to the root cellar.

Now return to the road and continue walking until, on your right, you'll notice an opening in the trees that is grass-covered, but wide enough for a car. *Don't drive down that road!* Walk down it, and you'll go in and down for a few minutes, until you'll see a narrow trail that goes off to your left toward the water. Just a short distance along that trail, and you are face-to-face with the remarkable four-foot-high stone wall surrounding the graves of John Robertson and his two wives. There are no gravestones inside, but the wall alone—deep in the woods—is worth the visit. Beyond this unique construction you'll see Black Cove through the trees. When you first see John Robertson's grave, if you look to your right you may be able to locate the broken head- and footstones of what is known as "the baby's grave."

Now re-trace your steps to the main road, and continue on until, at your right, a flat open field appears. In the centre, there's a huge rock and a plaque on that rock. This is the site of the Big Church to which people came from miles around to hear Reverend Norman McLeod preach. Behind the stone, through the alders and spruce, a moss-covered path invites you down along the slope to the headwaters of Black Cove. This is where the *Ark* anchored in 1821, bringing Norman and his followers to Cape Breton, and this is the shore where the *Margaret* was built—the first of six vessels that took followers of Norman McLeod from St. Ann's to New Zealand in 1851.

Appendix of Contemporary Voices

1

Gluskap's Journey

A Mi'kmaw Geography of St. Ann's Bay

In 1915 F. G. Speck took down a number of Cape Breton Mi'kmaq tales from the dictation of Chief Joe Julian of the Sydney band, and John Joe of Whycocomagh. They told him of the wonderful being, Gluskap. They told him:

One time when Gluskap had become the Indians' God, Christ wanted to try him to see if he was fit: so he took Gluskap to the ocean, and told him to close his eyes. Then Christ moved close to the shore an island which lay far out to sea. When Gluskap opened his eyes, he saw it. Christ asked him if he could do as much as that. Then Gluskap told Christ to close his eyes a while. When Christ opened his eyes, he found that Gluskap had moved it back to its place again.

Gluskap's Journey

Gluskap was the god of the Mi'kmaq. The great deity Ktc-ni'sxam made him out of earth and then breathed on him, and he was made. This was at Cape North, Cape Breton—on the eastern side. Gluskap's home was at Fairy Holes. Just in front of the caves at this headland are three little islands in a straight line, long and narrow, known as Ciboux Islands [today's Bird Islands]. These are the remains of Gluskap's canoe, where he left it when it was broken. At Plaster Cove

(Two'butc̀, "Looking Out") two girls saw his canoe broken into three pieces; and they laughed, making fun of Gluskap. At this he told them that they would forever remain where they are; and today there are two rocks at Plaster Cove which are the remains of these girls.

Next, a little farther north at Wreck Cove, Gluskap jumped from his canoe when it foundered, lifting his moose-skin canoe-mat out, and left it on the shore to dry. It is there today. There is still to be seen a space of fifteen acres of bare ground where the mat lay. Then he started on and went to Table Head (Padalodi'tck) on the south side of Great Bras d'Or. Here he had his dinner. Next he struck into Bras d'Or Lake straight to Whycocomagh, on the western end, where, at Indian Island (Wi'sik, "Cabin"), he started a beaver and drove him out, following Bras d'Or Lake to St. Patrick's Bay. At Middle River he killed a young beaver, whose bones are still to be seen there.

Then Gluskap followed the big beaver until he lost track of him for a while. He stood at Indian Island and took a piece of rock and threw toward the place where he thought the beaver was. This rock is now Red Island. This started the beaver up and he ran back through St. Peter's Channel and burrowed through underneath, which is the cause of the crooks and windings there now. Then the chase continued outside in the ocean, when the beaver struck out for the Bay of Fundy. Here at Pli'gank ("Split Place"), Split Point, Gluskap dug out a channel with his paddle, forming Minas Basin, Nova Scotia. There he killed the beaver. Near here is a small island, which is the pot in which he cooked the beaver; and there, too, is another rock near Pot Rock, which is Gluskap's dog, left behind at this time. Turtle (Mi'ktcik) was Gluskap's uncle. Here with his pot and dog he turned turtle into a rock and left them all there. Near where he killed the beaver are still to be seen the bones turned to rock. When he broke the channel to Minas Basin to drain the water out, in order to uncover the beaver, he left it so that today the water all drains out at each tide. So Gluskap caused the Bay of Fundy tides. Then he crossed over eastward and came out at Pictou, where there were many Indians living. While there, he taught the Mi'kmaq how to make all their implements for hunting and fishing—bows, arrows, canoes and the like.

After a while he prepared to leave, and told the Indians, "I am going to leave you. I am going to a place where I can never be reached by a white man." Then he prophesied the coming of the Europeans and the baptism of the Mi'kmaq. Then he called his grandmother from Pictou, and a young man for his nephew, and departed, going to the other side of the North Pole with them. Again he said, "From now on, if there should ever be a war between you and other people, I shall be back to help you."

He is there now, busy making bows, arrows and weapons for the day when the white man may bother the Mi'kmaq. The Mi'kmaq are Gluskap's children. As he prophesied it came true, for in 1610 the first Mi'kmaq were baptized and became Christians. Gluskap had departed just a little before them, because he knew he had to make room for Christ; but he is the Mi'kmaq's god and will come to help them if they ever need him. When Peary discovered the North Pole, he saw Gluskap sitting on top of the Pole, and spoke to him.

"Gluskap's Journey" includes mention of Fairy Holes, caves well-known by fishermen in St. Ann's Bay. Mr. Speck wrote that about 1860 "five Indians—Joe Bernard, Francis Bernard, Clement Bernard, Joe Newell and Tom Newell—entered the caves which honeycomb this headland, carrying seven torches. They walked as far as the torches would light them, about a mile and a half, found eight brooks in the caves, and when they came out discovered how a rock 300 feet wide had moved since they had entered. The Indians regard these caves as very mysterious."

Tommy Peggy MacDonald of the North Shore reported in the 1970s that people used to tell of a dog that went in the Fairy Holes and came out some days later at Ross Ferry—and when he came out the hair was all off him. Others told the sto-

ry, and although he was said to come out different places it was always without any hair.

F. G. Speck's interviews were first published in Journal of American Folklore *in 1915.*

2

Narrative of the Voyage undertaken by Captain Daniel from Dieppe to New France in 1629

On April 22, 1629, I took my departure from Dieppe by leave of Monseigneur the Cardinal de Richelieu, Grand Master, Chief and Superintendent-General of the Navigation and Commerce of France, in charge of the ships called the "Great St. Andrew" and the "Marguerite," for the purpose (pursuant to the order of Messieurs the Intendants and Directors of the Company of New France) of meeting the Commandant de Rasilly either at Brouage or Rochelle, and of thence proceeding under his escort to succour and carry provisions to M. de Champlain and the French who were in possession of the Fort and Settlement of Quebec in New France. On May 17, the day following our arrival at Ché de Boys, it was announced that peace had been made with the King of Great Britain. After remaining in the above named place for the space of thirty nine days, waiting for M. de Rasilly, but finding that he was not prepared to leave, and that the season was advancing for the undertaking of the said voyage: By the advice of the above named Directors, and without waiting any longer for M. de Rasilly, I took my departure from the roads of Ché de Boys on June 26, with four vessels and a barque belonging to the Company, and, pursuing my voyage as far as the Grand Bank, I encountered such stormy and foggy weather that I lost sight of my other vessels and was compelled to continue my voyage alone, until, being within about two leagues of the land, I perceived a ship with English colours hoisted, which ships, seeing that I carried no cannon, approached me within reach of pistol-shot, thinking that I was completely unprovided with ammunition. I then ordered the deck ports to be opened and a battery of sixteen cannon prepared for action. The Englishman becoming aware of this circumstance, endeavoured to escape, and I to pursue him, until, having approached him, I ordered him to haul down his colours whilst lying off coasts appertaining to the King of France, and to show me his commission, in order to ascertain if he was not a Pirate. Upon his refusal I ordered a few cannon shot to be fired, and boarded him. Having discovered that he was proceeding towards Cape Mallebarre with cattle and other things for some of his countrymen settled there, I informed him that as peace had been concluded between the two Crowns, he had nothing to fear, and might continue his voyage.

On August 28, I entered the river called by the Savages Great Cibou, and on the following day despatched a boat with ten men along the coast, to discover some Savages and learn from them the condition of the Settlement of Quebec. On arriving off Port Baleines, they found there a vessel from Bordeaux, the master of which was named Chambreau, who informed them that James Stewart, a Scotch Lord, had come there about two months previously with two large ships and an English cutter; that he had met in the said place Michael Dihourse of St. Jean de Luz engaged in fishing and drying Cod; that the said Scotch Lord had seized Dihourse's ship and cargo and had permitted his men to pillage the crew. Also that shortly after the said Lord had sent his two largest ships, with that taken from Michael Dihourse, to found a settlement at Port Royal [Historian Richard Brown added, "More probably with supplies and reinforcements for Sir William Alexander the younger, who settled at Port Royal in 1627"], and had with part of his men constructed a fort at Port aux Baleines. Further, that Stewart had given him a document signed with his own hand, purporting that he would not grant permission to him or any other Frenchmen to fish in future on the said coast or to traffic with the Savages, unless the tenth part of the profits were paid over to him; and that his Commission from the King of Great Britain authorised him to confiscate all vessels attempting to proceed to the above named places without his permission. These matters being reported to me, I considered that it was my duty to prevent the said Lord from usurping the country belonging to the King my master, and from exacting tributes from his subjects, which he intended to appropriate to himself. I therefore ordered 53 of my men to be well armed, and provided myself with ladders and other necessary materials for the siege and escalade of the said Fort. Having arrived on September 18 at Port Baleines, I landed at about two in the afternoon and ordered my men to advance towards the Fort according to the instructions I had given them, which were to attack on several sides with hand and pot grenades and other combustibles.

Notwithstanding the resistance made by the enemy, with the aid of musketry, after a time finding themselves closely pressed, they took alarm, and appeared on the parapets displaying a white flag and imploring for life and quarter from my lieutenant, whilst I made my way towards the gates of the Fort, which I promptly forced open, and, closely followed by my men, I entered and seized the above named Lord, whom I found armed with sword and pistol, surrounded by all his men, fifteen of whom were clothed in armour, each carrying a musket, the remainder armed with muskets and pikes only. Having disarmed these, I gave orders that the Banner of the King of England should be taken down and replaced by that of the King my master. I then searched the Fort, and there discovered a Frenchman, a native of Brest, whose name was Réné Cochoan, detained prisoner until his Captain (who had arrived two days previously at a port two leagues distant from Port Baleines) should bring a cannon which he had on board, and should pay the tenth of the fish he had taken.

On the following day I ordered a Spanish Caravel, which had run aground before the said Port, to be equipped and laden with the provisions and ammunition found in the Fort, which I caused to be razed to the ground, and the whole to be transported to the river of the Great Cibou, where I ordered 50 of my men and 20 Englishmen to work with the greatest diligence at the construction of an intrenchment or fort at the entrance of the above named river, so as to prevent the enemy from entering it. [Richard Brown: "The river of Great Cibou was undoubtedly St. Anne's Harbour. In Champlain's map, you will observe that Grand Cibou occupies the exact position of St. Anne's; and in many modern maps the Bird Islands, as they are now called, at the mouth of the bay, are styled the 'Ciboux Islands.' Captain Leigh, it is true, says in his journal that the savages called Sydney Harbour 'Cibo,' but this may have been a mistake; or, perhaps there were two harbours of that name—Cibou and Grand Cibou. Captain Daniel was probably the person who gave the name of St. Anne to Grand Cibou—the name which it retained until 1713, when the French called it Port Dauphin."]

I left as a garrison 40 men, including the Reverend Fathers Vimond and Vieupont, Jesuits, 8 pieces of cannon, 1,800 pounds of Powder, 600 matches, 40 muskets, 18 pikes, cannon and musket balls, provisions and all other things necessary, besides all that which had been found in the before named Fort of the English. Having hoisted the arms of the King and of Monseigneur the Cardinal, erected a house, chapel, and magazine, and having taken an oath of fidelity from the Sieur Claude, a native of Beauvais, whom I left there in command of the Fort and Settlement for the service of the King, and also the same oath from the men left in the above named place, I left on November 5 and brought with me the said Englishmen, women, and children, 42 of whom I landed near Falmouth, a seaport in England, with their clothes; the rest, 18 or 20, I brought to France, waiting the orders of Monseigneur the Cardinal. Which narrative I certify to be true, and to which I have appended my signature.

Paris, December 12, 1629.

Captain Daniel's above narrative is taken from Richard

Brown's A History of the Island of Cape Breton, *published in 1869. In it, Richard Brown continues:*

Such is Captain Daniel's story. To form a correct judgment, however, you must hear both sides of the question. The following is a verbatim copy of a Memorial upon the subject, presented by Lord Ochiltree to King James I., now in the Public Record Office in London:

3

Lord Ochiltree's Version, 1629

The Barbarous and perfidious cariage off the Frenche towards the Lord Wchiltrie in the Ile off Cap britaine proved in the Court off Admiralty off Deepe:

Aboutt the tent of Sep[r] or thereby on Captaine Daniell Induellar in Deepe accompanyed with three score soiours and ane certane number off Savages in six schallops cumis to the coast off Cap britane and surprysit too shallops and six fishermen in them who were at fishing for the intertinement off the sayd Lo. Wchiltrie his Colony in that part seattilt by wertew off the King off Brittane his commissione, having surprysed the schallops he seased upon the fishermen, and enclosed them in ane West Ile withoutt meatt drink fyr houses or any schelter from the rayne or cold. Therafter with his soiours and six schallops enterid the harborye the said Lo. Wchiltrie and the greatestt pertt off his men being abroad at bissiness.

The said Lo. Wchiltrie persaving them enterid his Forthe and with the few that wair in it esteming the said Captan Danyell and his people to have been Savages caused discharge sum muskattis att the schallops to mak them discover who they wer which did so fall furthe for they did immediatly approche the forthe and the said Lo. Wchiltrie finding by thayr apparell that they wer not savages did demand them who they wer they answered they were Frenche, he said the Frenche and they were freeinds because off the peace betwix the two kingis they replyed thatt they wer Frenche and thatt they did know the peace and wer thair freeinds then he said in theiar hearine they wer welcum how soone they did enter (expecting no wrong usage after the words which hayd past) they did seas on us all disarmed them entromittit with all thair goods expulsit the poor people outt off the forth and exposed them withoutt schelter or cover or clothis to the mercy off the rayne and cold wind which did exceed att that tym so yat the poor people (whereof ane greatt number of them wer old men and wemen with chyld and young childrein att thair breasts) they I say were forced to turned doune the face off ane old schallope and to creepe in under itt to save thayr lyffis from the bitterness off the cold and rayne which was most extreem in thatt place.

Therefter the said Captane Danyell and his people did enter the flea boatt which the said Lo. Wchiltrie hayd thayr seased upon all the goodis and immediately they did lavishly drink outt three hogsheads off wyne, too hogsheadis of strong ceadar and the whole beer which sould have served the people and did nocht reserve so muche as to save the sayd Lo. Wchiltrie and his people lyff in thayr jorney to France so that they wer all forced to drink stincking water to the Lo. Wchiltrie his greatt distemper by seckness and the loss off the lyffs of many of the people his Majesties subjecties.

They did take outt off the sayd Lo. Wchiltries schipe his Majesties collors and throw thayme under foott and did sett up the king off France collors with so much disdayne that the lyke hes nether beein seine nor red off in the tym of ane standing peace betwix two kings Efter some few dayis they did send away the most pertt of the said Lo. Wchiltrie his people in shallops some thretty league by sea to Schibo when the said captane Danyell his schipe did lye and all this thretty league did cause the poor people work at oareis as they hayd been slaves having no thing all this tym to live upone bott bread and water and many off them noct having clothes nather to cover their nackednes nor schelter them from the cold whatt greatter barbaryty could the Turke have used to Christians.

Efter some few dayes the said Lo. Wchiltrie with some too or thrie Ingliss gentlemen and thair wyffis wer caryed away in schalloups to the said Schiboa and for the tempestes of weather being forced to sett to the land at nycht they did ly upon the cold ground without schelter the rayne pouring downe upon them throche which unusuall distemper the said Lo. Wchiltrie did contract ane flux of blood which did continew with him for the space of fyve monthes which he is nocht yet lykely to scheack off.

Then he arrived at Schibo and howsoone Captaine Danyell cam to his schipe he did sett up the Kyng of Bretains collors on his schipe as a pryss ane actt unusuall in the tym of pace.

At Schibo for the space off sax or sevin weekis all the poor people wer compelled as slaves to work and labor upon bread and water only and many of them naked and without clothes so yatt for pitie of the poor people the sayd Lo. Wchiltrie was constrayned to give them his bed clothes to cover thair nackednes and saiff them in some measure from the extremitie of the cold and to tear the very lininge of his bed. When the said Lo. Wchiltrie and his people had indured this wrong and miserie for the space of two monthis, they were all imbarked in the said Captaine Danyells ship fyty men women and childrein being inclosed in the hold of the schipe in so little bound that they wer forced to ly upon other as they hayd beein so mony fisshes lying in thair awin filthe and fed upon bread and water That by famine and the pestiferus smell of thair awin filth many of them wer throwin in the sea throu famin the mothers lossing thair milk the poor souking childrein lost thair lyffe and wer throwin in the sea.

In this tym the said Lo. Wchiltrie distempered of ane flux of blood was for the compleaning of the people's usage threattnit to have his throatt cutt and to be pistolled his servant who did attend him in his seaknes discharged to cum to him to gitt him ane drink of water, his coffers where his clothes and his papers being only left unriffillid and unseasit upon till that tym wer taken and openit and his accuttances of great sowms of money wche he hayd payed obligationes of sowmis securities of his freinds lands wer taken by the said Captan Danyell and throwen in the sea.

And to crown the rest of the said Captn Danyells insolences before the Serjeant Major of Deepe Monsieur Schobneaw he did call the King of Britain ane usurpater.

In this action the said Lo. Wchiltrie hathe proven that pertly by the goods takin from him his lossis in his voyage and his loss by his accutances and wry-this which wer throwin in the sea he is losser above twenty thousand pounds starling.

This wholl relation the said Lo. Wchiltrie did prove before the Court of Admyraltie at Deepe procurit sentence upon itt and being keepit closs prisoner in Deepe for ane monthe by the means off his Majesties imbassador he was brocht to his hearing his offences against the King of France objected to him he defended himself by his Majesties Commission which he proved yat he navyr contrived nor transgressed and having no more to say against him he was delyvered to his Majesties imbassador he did present to the Consell his relation off his injuries and losses with the verification thereoff in the Court off Admiralty off Deepe the Judges sentence interposit thereto bot nether can he have his wronges repaired his lossis repayit nor the offender punished bot bi the contrarye the said Captan Danyell is imployed in new comission to go to America with on of the Kinge of France's shipis and to others to make good his possession of Cap Britan and the Ile of Cap Britan giving to him for his injuries done to the King of Britan and his subjects. Yea which is most barbarous and unjust the sentence of the Court of Admiraltie which he did present to the Consell of France is denyed to be given back to him it being so ordered as itt shamefull it suld be upon record so that the Lo. Wchiltrie is forced to have his recours to his Majestie whois humble desyr is "That his Majestie may be pleasit to tak his wrongis and losses to his princely and royall consideration and to be pleasit to provyd suche remead thereunto as in his Majesties unquestionable judgement will be found most fealt and for the truth of his relation he is content to answer it upon his lyff and in the mean tym doeth remitt the proff of it to the relation of Captane Constance Ferrer, Louetennant Tho. Maie Stewart, Hary Pew Gentleman and such others as theaie will find out who are witnissis in the said action and that his Majestie may be graciously pleasit to cause call them for the verification of theas relations in testimony of the treuth whereof the said Lo. Wchiltrie hath signed theas presentes."

J. L. Wchiltrie. [Ochiltree]

Captain Daniel's and Lord Ochiltree's versions of the attack on Baleine are taken from Richard Brown's A History of the Island of Cape Breton, *1869.*

4

Shipwreck at Canso, 1629

The following letter was written by Fr. Charles Lalemant, a survivor of the wreck at Canso. He tells of the disaster and of Fr. Vieuxport's leaving to serve the Indians at St. Ann's. It was Fr. Vieuxport, together with Fr. Vimont, who named the spot St. Ann's. This letter begins with the shipwreck. They were returning from a visit to France when they learned that Quebec had fallen to the English. In trying to sail back to France, they were caught in the storm. Fr. Lalemant's letter:

"The Lord chastising has chastised me; but he hath not delivered me over to death." (Psalms cxvii. 18) A chastisement the more severe, as the shipwreck has been attended by the death of the Rev. Father Philibert Noyrot, and of our brother, Louis Malot, two men who would, it seems to me, have been of great service to our seminary. Yet, as God has so disposed, we must seek consolation in his holy will, out of which there never was a solid or contented mind, and I am sure that experience has shown your reverence that the bitterness of our sorrows, steeped in the sweetness of God's good pleasure, when a soul binds itself indissolubly to that, loses all or most of its gall, or, if some sighs yet remain for past or present afflictions, it is only to aspire the more for heaven, and meritoriously perfect that conformity in which the soul has resolved to spend the rest of its days.

Of the four members of our Society in the ship, God, dividing equally, has taken two and left the two others. These two good religious, well disposed, and resigned to death, will serve as victims to appease God's wrath justly excited against us for our faults, and to render his goodness favorable henceforth to the success of our designs.

What destroyed our vessel was a violent southwester, which arose when we were off the coast; it was so impetuous that, with all the care and diligence of our captain and crew, with all the vows and prayers which we could offer to avert the blow, we could not avoid being driven on the rocks, on the 26th day after our departure, feast of St. Bartholomew, about 9 o'clock in the evening. Of twenty-four that were in the vessel, only ten escaped; the rest were engulphed in the waves. Father Noyrot's two nephews shared their uncle's fate. We interred the bodies of several, among others, of Father Noyrot and Brother Louis. Of seven others, we have had no tidings in spite of all our search.

To tell you how Father Vieuxport and I escaped, would be difficult, and I believe that God alone knows, who, according to the designs of his divine providence, has preserved us; for, for my own part, not deeming it possible, humanly speaking, to avoid the dangers, I had resolved to stay in the cabin with Brother Louis, preparing ourselves to receive the death stroke, which could not be delayed over three *Misereres*, when I heard some one calling me on deck. Supposing that my assistance was needed, I ran up and found that it was Father Noyrot, who asked me to give him absolution. After giving it, and singing the *Salve Regina* with him, I had to stay on deck; for there was no way to get below; for the sea was so high and the wind so furious, that, in less than a moment, the side on the rock went to pieces. I was close by Father Noyrot when a wave broke so impetuously against the side where we were standing, that it dashed it to pieces, and separated me from

Father Noyrot, from whose lips I heard these last words: "Into thy hands I commend my spirit." For my own part, this same wave left me struggling amid four fragments of the wreck, two of which struck me so violently on the chest, and the other two on the back, that I expected to be killed before sinking forever; but, just then, another wave disengaged me from the fragments, sweeping off my cap and slippers, and scattered the rest of the ship over the sea. I fortunately fell on a plank to which I clung; it was connected with the rest of the side of the ship.

There we were then at the mercy of the waves, which did not spare us, rising I cannot tell how many feet above our heads, and then breaking over us. After floating thus a long while in the dark, for night had set in, I perceived, on looking around me, that I was near the shore of what seemed to be an island, which almost surrounded us, and was covered with brambles. Looking a little more attentively, I made out six persons not far from me, two of whom perceiving me, urged me to do my best to join them; this was not easy, for I was greatly enfeebled by the blows I had received from the fragments of the wreck. I exerted myself, however, so much that, by the help of my planks, I at last reached them, and by their aid got on the mainmast, which was still fast to part of the ship. I was not here long; for, as we got nearer the island, our sailors quickly got ashore, and, by their help, all the rest of us were soon there.

There we were, seven in all; I had no hat or shoes; my cassock and clothes all torn, and my body so bruised that I could scarcely stand up, and, in fact, they had to support me to enable me to reach the wood. I had two severe contusions on the legs, especially the right one, which is still painful; my hands cloven open and bruised; my hip torn, and my chest much injured.

We now retired to the wood wet as we came from the sea. Our first care was to thank God for preserving us, and to pray for those who were lost. That done, we lay down close by each other in order to try and get warm, but the ground and the grass, still wet with the heavy rain, was not much fitted to dry us. Thus we spent the rest of the night, during which Father Vieuxport, who, thank God, was unhurt, slept well.

The next morning, at daybreak, we began to examine the spot where we were, and found it to be an island from which we could pass to the main land. On the shore we found many things that the sea had thrown up; among which I picked up two shoes, a cap, hat, cassock, and other necessary articles. Above all, Providence sent us, in our want, five kegs of wine, ten pieces of pork, oil, bread, cheese, and a gun and powder, which enabled us to strike a fire. After we had thus gathered all we could, on St. Louis' day, all set to work to do their best to build a boat out of fragments of the wreck, in which to coast along till we found a fishing-smack. We set to work with the wretched tools we found, and it was pretty well advanced on the fourth day, when we perceived a craft sailing towards the spot where we were. They took on board one of our sailors, who swam out near to where they were passing, and took him to their captain. That worthy man, hearing of our misfortunes, let down his boat, and came ashore to offer us a passage. We were thus saved; for, the next day, we all slept on board. It was a Basque vessel, fishing about a league and a half from the rock where we struck, and, as their fishing season was far from being gone, we stayed with them the rest of August and all the month of September.

On the first of October, an Indian came to tell the captain that, if he did not sail, he ran a risk of being taken by the English. This news made him give up his fishing, and prepare for the voyage home. The same Indian told us that Captain Daniel was building a house twenty-five leagues off, and had some Frenchmen there with one of our fathers. Father Vieuxport had already pressed me very hard to let him stay with this Indian, who was really one of the best that could be found. I now told him, "Here, father, is a means of satisfying your reverence. Father Vimont will not be sorry to have a companion. This Indian offers to take you to Daniel's place; if you wish to stay there, you may; if you wish to spend a few months with the Indians and learn the language, you may do so, and both Father Vimont and yourself will be satisfied." The good father was quite delighted at the opportunity, and set off in the Indian's canoe. I let him have all we had saved, except the large painting which our Basque captain had taken, and which I would have made him give up, if another disaster had not befallen us.

We left the coast on the sixth of October, and after more violent storms than I had yet ever seen, on the fortieth day of our voyage, as we were entering a port near San Sebastian in Spain, we were a second time wrecked. The vessel went into a thousand pieces, and all the fish was lost. All that I could do was to get into a boat in slippers and nightcap as I was, and, in that guise, go to our Father's at San Sebastian. I left there a week after, and, on the 20th of the present month, reached Bourdevac, near Bordeaux.

Such was the issue of our voyage, by which you may see how great reason we have to be thankful to God.

Charles Lalemant, S. J.

Bordeaux, November 22, 1629.

This letter was translated by John Gilmary Shea from Champlain's 1632 Voyages.

5

A Letter from St. Ann's Bay, 1634

A letter sent by Father Julien Perrault, of the Society of Jesus, to his Provincial, in France, in the years 1634 and1635.

The Island of Cape Breton is about nine hundred leagues distant from our France by sea. It is seventy or eighty leagues in circumference. The mountains here are very high and numerous, at the foot of which are seen great bogs and frightful precipices. The land is covered with all sorts of trees, such as oak, beech, birch, pine, hemlock, and others.

Chibou (St. Ann's Bay), which is the principal part of

this Island, is a great Bay about two leagues wide at its entrance, becoming narrower little by little, in the six or seven leagues which form its extent. In the middle, on the left hand in ascending, on the summit of the shore that faces the Northwest, is built the fort of sainte Anne, at the entrance of the harbor, opposite a little Cove. The situation of the place is so advantageous, according to the report of those who are acquainted with it, that with ten or twelve pieces of cannon, all the hostile ships that might present themselves could be sent to the bottom.

Those who have grown old upon the sea protest that they have never seen a more desirable Port, either in extent or for its facility of access. Three thousand ships could easily anchor there, and be sheltered from every wind, in a beautiful enclosure very pleasant to look upon; for its form is circular, or nearly so. The tides here are very mild and regular; there is always from ten to twelve fathoms of water. Furthermore, notwithstanding that the Island is in forty-six and a half degrees north latitude, the cold is extreme, the island lying in the midst of snow five or six months of the year. This is the situation of the place, let us come to the conveniences of life which it offers to its inhabitants. On this subject we may say, in general, that the Savages are more comfortable here than in many other places. If the Winter supplies them with fewer Beavers upon the water, it gives them, by way of compensation, more Moose upon the land. In summer, they live very well on Marmots and Parrot fish, with Cormorants and other marine birds. They have also Bustards, Smelts, Mackerel, Codfish, and like supplies, according to the different seasons, in the forests or upon the coasts of the sea.

As to the people, there is nothing anomalous in their physical appearance; you see well-formed men, good-looking, of fine figures, strong and powerful. Their skin is naturally white, for the little children show it thus; but the heat of the Sun, and the rubbing with Seal oil and Moose fat, make them very swarthy, the more so as they grow older. Most of them go bare-headed, and they have long, black hair, with very little or no beard, so that the women cannot be distinguished, except that they use a girdle and are less naked than the men; quite the reverse of what is practiced in many Christian lands, to the shame of Christianity. One sees there old men, of eighty and a hundred years, who have hardly a gray hair. As to their intelligence, if we may judge from their conduct and from their way of dealing with the French, they are not at a great disadvantage. You do not see in their gestures and bearing any foolishness or nonsense, but rather a certain gravity and natural modesty, which makes them agreeable. They are indeed so clever that, in order to disguise their language, they add to every word a syllable, which only serves to confuse the minds of those by whom they do not wish to be understood.

What they do lack is the knowledge of God and of the service that they ought to render to him, as also of the state of the soul after death; it is wonderful that we have not yet been able to discover any trace of this knowledge in what we know of their language. Perhaps we shall discover something more, when we become better versed in it; for it is not credible that the light of nature should be altogether extinct in them in this regard, when it is not in other more barbarous Nations, or that they never talk among themselves of that of which they cannot be entirely ignorant. For all that, we have not up to the present noticed any more Religion among these poor Savages than among brutes. This is what wrings our hearts with compassion for souls redeemed at the same price as ours, by which they would willingly profit better than we, if they could know what they themselves are worth, and what they cost him who has loved us all so much.

Now what consoles us in the midst of this ignorance and barbarism, and what makes us hope some day to see the Faith widely planted, is partly the docility they have shown in wishing to be instructed, and partly the honesty and decency we observe in them.

They are very diligent and attentive to the instructions we give them; I do not know whether it is through complaisance, for they have a great deal of this naturally, or through an instinct from above, that they listen to us so willingly concerning the mysteries of our Faith, and repeat after us, whether they understand it or not, all that we declare to them. They very willingly make the sign of the Cross, as they see us make it, raising their hands and eyes to Heaven and pronouncing the words, "Jesus, Mary," as we do—so far that, having observed the honor we render to the Cross, these poor people paint it on their faces, chests, arms, and legs, without being asked to do so. I am very willing that they should do all these things in the beginning from a natural simplicity, which causes them to imitate all they see, rather than from any greater consideration; because in time they may be helped by it, and they will not be the first, who come to practice by choice that to which by casual encounter they have become accustomed. Besides, what is of no small importance, they sometimes urge us to pray our good Jesus for them, for the success of their hunting and for relief from their diseases.

The other encouragement we see here, for the preaching of the Gospel, is in the honesty and decency that we see shining forth in them like two bright rays of light in the midst of darkness. We never think of distrusting our Savages, or of watching their hands and their feet, as with some others who attract everything to them and appropriate all they find at their convenience. Everything is free to them in all places, and yet nothing is in danger in their presence, even if they are alone in a cabin and where no one can see them. As to decency, they hold it in such high estimation, at least as far as external appearances are concerned, in their actions and words, that there is a probability that they will rise up on the last day and condemn many Christians, who will have cultivated this virtue less under the Law of grace, than these poor people have under that of nature.

We have never heard them use unseemly words, nor seen any actions too free, although we have lived on familiar terms with them inside and outside their cabins.

You would say they are trying to practice in advance

that beautiful motto of the Apostle, which commands Christians not even to have, if they can help it, upon their lips a word which signifies indecency. Some one will readily reply that, if we were better versed in their language, we would not fail to notice it therein. But is it not a great deal, that the little we know of it has not taught us anything of the kind? And is there not great reason to blush for many Christian Nations, among whom one does not have to serve a long apprenticeship to their Grammar, to find oneself embarrassed and confused in company, if he has even a little regard for propriety? And if our ears are not yet sufficiently opened to give positive evidence of the unconcern or decency of their talk; are we blind, or are we incapable of recognizing a shameful gesture or action? And yet we have never seen anything of this kind, not even among married people. But what shall I say about noticing one day a young Savage kissing a woman, who I did not think was his wife; as that seemed something extraordinary among them, I straightway asked him if that was his wife, and he replied that she was; but it was not without embarrassment on the part of the two who had been taken by surprise. Add to this modesty the gravity which I have said is natural to them, and you will judge that, God helping, they will receive with open arms a Law which recommends nothing so much as this virtue, which makes men like unto Angels; and that they will not have as much difficulty as many badly taught Christians have, to conform entirely to the injunctions of the Gospel, when it shall be declared to them in the words of the Apostle that they have to show their modesty in the eyes of all the world, since the Lord is near. It is true they have polygamy, and pay no attention to the indissolubility of Marriage. But we must hope that, when they come to recognize the obligations they are under, together with all the Nations of the earth, to a God who made himself man for them, they will willingly submit to his most holy Laws, especially in that which concerns a virtue by means of which he wishes us to bear witness to and glorify without ceasing, in our bodies, him who for us has delivered his own up to torture, and who gives it to us every day as food, for this sole purpose.

This letter from St. Ann's Bay is "Relation de quelques particularitez, du lieu & des Habitans de l'Isle du Cap Breton," and is taken from Volume 8 of the 73-volume book The Jesuit Relations and Allied Documents, Travels and Explorations of the Jesuit Missionaries in New France, 1610-1791, in the Original French, Latin, and Italian Texts, with English Translations and Notes, *edited by Reuben Gold Thwaites.*

6

Fr. Pacifique's "Early History of St. Ann's" (Englishtown), 1930

An address by Rev. Fr. R. P. Pacifique at St. Ann's, C. B., August 25th, 1930, on the occasion of the unveiling of a Cairn with Tablet under the auspices of the Historic Sites and Monuments Board.

There is a well known short maxim used as a kind of watchword in my province of Quebec, "I do remember," meaning that we must have in our mind the glories of the past and also the lessons thereof. Now, if TO REMEMBER were a privilege of Quebec, we should say today that here we are in a distant corner of it. But no, there is no need to be a citizen of Quebec to remember. Men like Judge Crowe and other worthy members of the Historic Sites and Monuments Board of Canada can well compete with any French Canadian, not only to remember but to make others remember.

We are here for the dedication of a tablet prepared by them—an engraved Remembrance—purporting to mark one of the oldest historic sites of the country, and to recall significant events of our early history.

The tablet states first that this place WAS ESTABLISHED IN 1629. This is true, exactly true. It we know. We have not to say "about" or "likely" or "maybe." There is no fancy here, no probability; we have plain documents.

So 301 years ago—this is a long time for a young country—this very month of August, the 28th day, like next Thursday, a French captain, Charles Daniel, of Dieppe, entered with his crew this bay and harbour. The bay was called at the time Chibou, or Grand Chibou, an Indian word meaning river; but the Indians themselves called it, and call it still, by quite a different name, Mtjegatitjg, of which they don't care to give the meaning.

It was not there that Daniel was sent, nor to Bay of Baleines, both unknown to him, but to Quebec with provisions and dispatches. It was a heavy storm which parted him from his companions on the banks of Newfoundland and threw his ship on the eastern shore of Cape Breton. I say this because some French writers have blamed him for staying here, where he had no errand entrusted to him, instead of going to Quebec. But he does not deserve the blame. He repaired here on account of the storm; and the next day he sent ten men into the country to seek some Indians and then received the very sad information that not only were many English men-of-war in the St. Lawrence River, but also that the city had been captured by Kirke one month previous (July 19, 1629); so it was useless and very dangerous for him to go there just to be caught by them. So he stayed here and did well.

Then he was informed by the same Indians and some French fishermen that an English or Scotch gentleman, Sir James Stewart, or Lord Ochiltree, had fortified himself with about sixty men in the Bay of Baleines (present-day Baleine), on the south shore of the Island; that he had seized or ransacked some French ships; was charging a tax on fishing and trading with Indians.

Daniel, who was a member of the French company—one of the Hundred Associates—deemed it his duty to interfere, and in case of resistance to attack and destroy the English fort. So he did on the 8th of September. (Champlain says on the 18th, but it is surely a mistake or misprint, as the date is plainly stated not only by J. Felix, the writer, in "Relation of Daniel," but by Ochiltree himself, who states in his report that the fort was taken about the 10th of September, and so we may safely say it was attacked on the 8th and captured on the 9th or 10th.) There were very few casualties though the fort was destroyed, and men and supplies were carried to Grand Chibou; but none was molested in his person or personal goods. The English authorities in London had not much to say about that event. Only late in the winter the King mentioned that the capture had taken place—after the signing of the treaty of Sousa, April 24th; but as the capture of Quebec had taken place in the same crucial circumstances, and was of quite another importance, no more was said of Bay of Baleines.

Daniel built another fort here and put on it the arms of the French King and Cardinal Richelieu. He built also a house, a store and a chapel. My learned friend, Dr. Ganong, sums up in these words the whole affair:

"On the commanding high land on the south side of the entrance is an old fort site, the only one known around the harbor. It was there, as the Jesuit Relations clearly show, that Captain Daniel built his fort in 1629, as related by Champlain, and here, after 1713, was built the Fort Dauphin, contemporary of Louisbourg, as shown on Charlevoix's detailed plan, and of which traces still remain. Considering the commanding position of the site, its convenience to the fishery, including a fine, great drying beach opposite, the lack of any other known early French site about the harbor, the presence of early clearings and defences, and the concurrence of cultivated land close by, it seems altogether likely that the Simon Denys establishment, which was founded about 1650, stood here.... Of course all traces of it were obliterated by the building of Fort Dauphin on the same site."

When his fort was well on the way to completion, Captain Daniel left it in charge of his lieutenant, Gaulde or Claude of Beauvais, with a garrison of 40 men, including two Jesuit Fathers, and started for France on the 5th of November.

This brings us to the second statement on the Memorial

Tablet: It was THE SITE OF AN EARLY JESUIT MISSION.

One Jesuit Father, Bartholomew Vimont, came with Daniel and was the very first known missionary that landed on what is now Cape Breton. He had been Rector of the Jesuit College at Vannes. A companion was brought to him in a very tragical manner.

The same storm that had thrown Daniel's ship on this shore had, a few days before, thrown on the rocks of Canso another ship on which was another Jesuit Father, Father Noyrot, who had with him three other members of his order, and many passengers, all bound to Quebec. They were shipwrecked on August 24th at nine o'clock in the evening. Two fathers were drowned and two saved—Father Lallemant, the Superior of the Canadian Missions, and Father de Vieuxpont. This one asked his Superior the permission to spend the winter with some Indians whom they had met. One of them informed them that Daniel was building a fort twenty-five leagues from the place of shipwreck and offered to take the Father there in his canoe. The offer was accepted and they left Canso on the 6th of October. Father Lallemant returned to France with some Basque fishermen.

We may imagine how great was the joy of Father Vimont to receive a companion so unexpectedly in so remote a place. It was those two fathers who gave the place the name of St. Anne's—not surely to imitate St. Anne de Beaupré, which was not established until twenty-nine years later, nor St. Anne d'Auray in Brittany, whose sanctuary was just opened the year previous, but undoubtedly in pursuance of a recommendation of the pious Queen Anne of Austria, mother of Louis XIV.

This was the very first church named thus and dedicated to that glorious saint in North America. There were two or three St. Anne's in South and Central America before this St. Anne's in Cape Breton. There are now thirty-seven churches in Canada and twenty-eight in the United States which followed this one and are named after the saint.

During the first winter both missionaries had much to

do. The dreadful disease of scurvy made its appearance and Father Vimont had a hard task to attend the sick, watch the dying, bury the dead. Twelve men died during the winter and are buried somewhere here under our feet, which makes the place more pathetic, not to say more sacred. Father de Vieuxpont spent the winter in the woods, as he had wished, with the Indians, who became so fond of him that they readily brought to him their children to be baptized, and invited him to their camps.

These were the same class of missionaries that their brethren of Nova Scotia had seen and heard and loved at Port Royal in 1611. Their mission there had been short, being destroyed by Argall in 1613; but it was long enough to win to themselves the heart of this interesting tribe, who readily called their teaching the "Doctrine of the Black Robes"—"Magtaoegenagaoei"—and call it thus still.

After the Jesuit Fathers there came to Port Royal, now Annapolis, Franciscan Fathers, called at that time Recollets, in 1619; then Capuchin Fathers in 1632, another branch of the same order, to which your humble speaker has the honor to belong. These had a house at St. Peter's and may have come here occasionally after the departure of the Jesuit Fathers. Naming what first struck their sight, the simple children of the forest called their teaching the "Doctrine of the Bare Feet"—"Sesagigeoei"—and still use the same word. Of course they knew it was the Doctrine of Christ, the Christian Doctrine—"Alasotmamgeoei"—but delivered unto them by those two classes of their pioneer missionaries.

Two or three events of the first year of St. Anne's Mission, as told by the pious Malapart, a companion of the Captain, may prove of interest. He thought they were due to the merits of the missionaries, and there is of course nothing impossible therein, and we have an eye-witness.

In a cruise, he says, our men were in such danger that all prepared for death; but one of the fathers, having cast into the raging sea a relic of the Holy Cross, there came a great calm. Another time an Indian boy, grievously wounded on the head with an axe, was blessed by another father and perfectly healed.

But a spiritual healing more important was the conversion of an old medicine man, ninety years of age, who was like the high priest of those pagan Indians. So thoroughly was he changed that he would destroy by fire all his superstitious articles. We may hail him as the first convert of St. Anne in Cape Breton, a worthy follower of Membertou, the first convert of the whole tribe in Port Royal twenty years before. Unfortunately, the name of this one is not given, but as Membertou was a title rather than a personal name (meaning general leader), so we could, if my Micmac friends had no objection, quite properly give him that name, "Gtjpoooin"—"the Great Wizard."

The first two missionaries stayed at St. Anne's only one year and then returned to France like their companions at Quebec.

During their and the Captain's absence a very sad event occurred, which reminds us of the crime which stained the foundations of ancient Rome, when one of the founders was murdered by his brother. Gaulde had a very bad temper and could not get along with Martel, his assistant. It became evident that the latter should be recalled to France, and so it was decided, but not before the Captain's return. Gaulde, however, had not the patience to wait, and one evening after supper—on Pentecost Monday, 1631—he went into the fort whilst Martel was playing outside in the bowling alley, took his rifle, fired at him and killed him. Of course the Captain would have punished him according to his desert, but he made his escape into the country at once.

This and other hardships caused the poor colony to long for the return of Daniel and the Missionaries. The former was back on the 26th of June, but for a very short time. His brother Andrew was with him, and he left him in charge of the fort and again crossed the ocean. After the Treaty of St. Germain-en-Laye (1632), which restored Canada to France, he returned for the third time, bringing with him two other

Jesuit Missionaries. One of them was his own brother, Father Antoine Daniel, who was to be later one of the holy Canadian martyrs murdered by the Iroquois July 4, 1648; the other was Father Devost. They remained here till May, 1633, when Champlain, returning to Quebec, called at St. Anne's and carried them with him to the Capital.

Two others came in 1634, Father Richard and Father Perrault, and in 1636 Father George d'Endeman. These were the seven pioneer Missionaries of St. Anne's; indeed, the only ones that were resident here. Father Perrault wrote a very interesting and long relation of what he saw during his short stay [see this Appendix page 144]. He praises greatly the natural qualities of the Indians. He says that they are faithful, honest and modest in their behavior. Seeing once a young man who gave a kiss to a young woman, and knowing that they don't practice such familiarities before being married, he asked the young man if she was his wife. He answered that she was, each humbly blushing for his suspicion. For these and other qualities Father Perrault thought they were likely to receive willingly the Christian doctrine as soon as the Missionaries were able to teach them. Seeing the French forming the sign of the cross on their breast, they tried to do the same, very respectfully, guessing that there must be a deep meaning in such a simple ceremony, and to pronounce the holy names of Jesus and Mary.

From their intercourse with the French at St. Anne's they derive that devotion, let us say love, that fondness for the gracious saint whom they call their Grandmother and their Queen. They always celebrate her feast most solemnly. When there was no longer any mission here they repaired to Malagawatch and then to Chapel Island, where they continue meeting.

The Jesuit Mission at St. Anne's came to an end in 1641, when Father Richard was sent to Miscou, though the place continued to be visited occasionally until 1660. After the departure of the Missionaries the other settlers left also; but Simon Denys, whose brother Nicholas was at St. Peter's, established there a farm and fishery. He had his sixth child born here in 1651 and baptized under the name of Marguerite. But Le Borgne, a tradesman of La Rochelle, seized their property as a would-be creditor of D'Aulnay. This right, however, was not recognized in France, and he was bound to give it back when Nicholas Denys was appointed in 1654 a general grantee and governor of the whole coast. Curiously enough, the capture of Port Royal by the English did not molest them in the least. Simon's grandson, Denys de la Ronde, Captain of Infantry, 1713, was told by the Indians that his grandfather had at St. Anne's cultivated fields and orchards—he saw some apple trees himself and picked good apples.

He was still at St. Anne's in 1659, but afterwards we know nothing of the place. In a census of 1686 there is not one European family mentioned in the whole Island of Cape Breton. In a report of September 9th, 1713, signed by the new French Governor, Saint Ovide, and Father de la Marche, Superior of the Recollet Fathers, also by La Ronde Denys, they stated that at their arrival they found only one French family and twenty-five or thirty Indian families.

We come now to the last part of the inscription, which is the longest on the tablet, but my comment thereon will be the shortest. It reads: "Selected, 1713, as a naval base, and one of the principal places in Isle Royale; named Port Dauphin and strongly fortified. Its importance declined with the choice, 1719, of Louisbourg as the capital."

After the Treaty of Utrecht the necessity of a strong naval station in Cape Breton was evident, but much consideration was given to the choice of a site, and there was much hesitation between St. Anne's and Havre à l'Anglais, on the south shore. Denys de la Ronde sent a report to the Minister of Marine strongly recommending the former, which he called the most beautiful harbor in the world, far better than Havre à l'Anglais, recommended by others. This one, however, was chosen by the local authorities and the choice was approved by the King (Louis XIV) on January 26th, 1714, and the troops were sent there. The publisher of Daniel's "Relation" says that it was a mistake to have preferred it, the ground being not so good to cultivate and much more expensive to fortify. This last consideration became so evident that both the authorities and the King changed their minds and decided for St. Anne's as the principal establishment, without leaving Louisbourg. The English Governor at Annapolis remarked sadly in 1715, Nov. 23rd, "the regulars are moved to St. Peter's and St. Anne's to work on the fortifications, and that there is a very great resort of traders there from all parts of France." The fact that he does not name Louisbourg at all shows that it was then definitely left in the background.

This was the new name given to Havre à l'Anglais when chosen in 1714; St. Anne's was called Port Dauphin; St. Peter's, Port Toulouse, and the whole Island, Isle Royale. But those names did not last very long, except Louisbourg, and especially did St. Anne send away the Dauphin, leaving to him only a cape at the entrance of the bay. Some years after the English tried to change the name of the harbor into Conway Harbour, which she did not like any better, and left to him also a small point and retook to herself bay, harbour, mountain and post office. And nobody regrets it today. Even those who would not venerate her as a saint cannot help appreciating her as a beautiful historical character and a model to mothers.

Its importance declined after 1719, but continued to have a regular religious service held by the Recollets from Louisbourg. In 1753 it was a Father Julian that ministered at St. Anne's. A garrison continued also to occupy the fort. Captain Dangeac, the glorious defender of our own Ristigouche fort, was sent there in 1744 with provisions for one year. It was not molested at the first fall of Louisbourg, nor at the second; it was never taken by the English, but passed into their hands by virtue of the capitulations of Montreal in 1760, whereby all French establishments in North America passed to the British Crown. (Since writing this I read a paper by my friend Dr. Webster, stating that St. Anne's and

Espagnol [Sydney] were occupied. He must have good ground for saying so, and I accept his statement.)

The French disappeared altogether and the fort went into ruin, St. Anne's Chapel also. Vernon says, "These ruins may still be traced. The bell used at this church was found a number of years ago and carried to the United States." I tried to trace it, if not to get it, but without success.

Today, if we still see only these ruins, they will now be linked to a glorious, often heroic, past by the attention of the present settlers and visitors, for whom the Memorial Tablet will stamp out forgetting.

This address was first published in The Cape Breton Historical Society: Some Papers and Records of the Society 1928 to 1932.

7

The Burning of St. Ann's Bay, 1745

Here is an extract from Rev. Adonijah Bidwell's diary, kept when the New Englanders besieged Louisbourg. It's a description of the Destruction of St. Ann's.

May 17 In ye morning we anchored at ye south end of this large bay,...St. Anns Bay. In ye afternoon we sailed several miles up the bay to a narrow Strait there were several houses on the east side.... We anchored and several men went on shore.

May 18 This day ye men ransacked ye town & woods, burnt ye town of about 20 houses & about ye same number of shallops, took 12 or 15 Feather Beds, 3 or 4 cases with bottles, Chests with Cloths, Iron Pots, Brass Kittles, Candlesticks, Frying Pans, Pewter Plates & Spoons etc. took one prisoner....

May 20 Two boyes went on shore up Angonish Bay & burnt a Town of about 80 houses which stood up that bay, about noon stear'd for Louisbourg.

Rev. Bidwell's diary appears in the New England Historical & Genealogical Register.

8

Letters of Rev. Norman McLeod 1835-1851

St. Ann's Cape Breton 31st Decr 1835
Dear Friends

Your letter dated 1st Septr. came to hand in due course. It would be ungrateful in me not to feel sincerely glad for the account you gave of the state of our kind friends in that quarter.... There is no particular change among us, but that two of our Settlers have lately gone to see Canada, in hopes of meeting some encouragement for settling in that country. The individuals are Norman McDonald & Alexr. Munro both sons-in-law to Duncan Munro Caraboo. This settlement would indeed be better of wanting these men with their families, & a few other persons that will be apt to accompany them, in any case they may find places elsewhere any way suitable to their wishes. You know that McDonald has been for many years dissatisfied, on religious accounts, and for a long time promised himself to gain a strong party to strengthen his foolish pretensions; but by degrees failing of success, and more desperately of late, he thought proper at last to abandon this quarter. As to Munro his discontent originated & ripened mainly from dire misunderstanding arising and existing between his family & some of his nearest relations around him; especially for dexterous deceit & falsehood in his children, supported by their mother, & neither acknowledged nor corrected by him, till he tired the patience of his dearest neighbours and best friends, so that his own very brothers, who perhaps have been too indulgent & patient to him, were notwithstanding obliged to engage another Schoolmaster, even a mere new emigrant, in his stead, before he left this place. We were since a long time desirous to be rid of such malcontents as these in question, whenever it would fall out in the course of providence. Other friendly people are glad to purchase their Lots, & settle in their places. Dond Fraser from West

Branch bought McDonald's land which you know is opposite the point of mine. Little do they conceive what mercies & privileges they exchange for wild Canada, where, according to a late calculation, there are ten Romanists to every Protestant, and the latter too frequently also of indifferent characters and various persuations, besides many other exceptions. Were there no fatality or demerit in sin but what is incurred thro the influence thereof, even in this life it would be indeed alarming to any enlightened mind.

St. Ann's C.B. 15th June, 1839

I do not see reason to trouble you or myself in detailing secular concerns of no great importance, especially since the bearer can inform you of any such matters. And what shall I say of religious subjects, since the times are so fearfully dark & dead! And if your souls felt the dangers of such dreadful signs as are now visible in the religious world, it would be likely to make you break silence in some manner or other; especially, as your quarter of the Country seems to be in as deplorable a condition on that ground, as any part around. It is likely you are, at best, but weakly affected for the Lord's manifest and fearful withdrawings of his spiritual communications from communities & individuals. This judgement, my friends, is the most direful & dangerous in the world; and yet generally the least lamented among almost all mankind; and particularly those more deeply under its destructive power. A degree of mere morality, or formal devotion will not exempt Societies, or particular members from this fatal frown of Heaven. O, my correspondents, what can I write on this most solemn & interesting theme! The Sovereign Lord & Governor of the Universe has left men under the power of delusive opinions, & deadly sleep on this awful ground, crying peace, peace, when there is no peace. The soul that is not affected or alarmed now on this dreadful point is manifestly under the sad dominion of spiritual death & delusion. It is the Lord's powerful operation upon the heart & conscience that can properly & effectually arouse men to a dire sense of this most serious & important subject. Mere profession, dead devotion, & an outward rusty shell of religion, without tenderness of conscience, life of affection, or renovation of spirit, are the open and gloomy plague of our day; and if you had any spark of life awake in your souls, you would fear your situation & fellowship, as the very brink of ruin without lively means of teaching & discipline, and a conscientious example according to the spirit of the Gospel of Jesus Christ.

St. Ann's, C.B. 10th March, 1840

O, the hateful pride & rank obstinacy—the deep-rooted worldliness & dreadful malignity—the secret contempt of God & of good men, with all their direful train of concomitants that are hiddenly lurking & domineering in the breast of every carnal and unregenerated man in the world! And these & similar vices are excited and break forth into practice in less or greater degrees, according to the different inclinations & circumstances of men, and the various temptations to which from day to day they are exposed. I do not by any means choose to discourage your correspondence; but allow me in humility and meekness to observe that your letters in general are marked with a dangerous degree of deadness & unconcern. You seem to be slumbering under the fatal power of spiritual sleep: so that I am actually & earnestly ashamed to show or to read them to our very friends & serious well wishers. But if I were even present with you, I would indeed feel afraid to speak to some of you on the particular grounds of your spiritual maladies in an explicit & unreserved manner according to my humble & familiar knowledge....

I do not know the comparison of Pictou in the whole land, for shameless & daring wickedness.... I humbly desire to bless the name of the Lord, for having given me and some of my (friends) a gate to escape from it in time; tho' I deeply regret that others, of my kind fellow creatures, are left behind under such deplorable unconcern about themselves & others in the middle of a branch of Sodom. I (say) Sodom, particularly in reference to the places about N. Glasgow; for besides other points of extravagance, I have (heard from) eyewitnesses of the filthiness prevalent there, particularly at the shipping places, where it is customary to see (word obliterated) accompany sailors during the night.... O! Pictou, Pictou! Thy sins are fearful and thy judgements are alarming...if I could treat of it in humility I would tell you that I see reason to bless the Lord for having ordered my lot in this very spot. Whatever causes of complaint we may think to have in this life yet when I seriously endeavour to draw comparisons between different places I verily believe upon very sure grounds that we are in a certain degree behind the storm; and in many instances enjoy privileges both negative & positive beyond most places in the world....

St Ann's C.B. 1st Feby 1846

In reference to the books [Rev. McLeod's book, published late 1843, *The Present Church of Scotland and a Tint of Normanism contending in a Dialogue*], unless friendly persons should choose to buy them, I had no great expectation of prejudiced people in their favor. You wrote that they were objected to, by many, on account of the severity of the writing; and so they may; but this generation is proportionately severe against Heaven; and that under the mask of friendship and devotion.... I sorely regret to live in a generation so hardened and aggravated against means of knowledge as to require such severity; but who can help it. We must act and work according to the requisition of the spirit of our time.... Whatever the publication may do there, or in any other quarter, (blessed) be the Lord's name, it has done a good deal of service in Cape Breton by muzzelling the mouths of many objectors, & slanderers, moderating the vicious reflections of others, and gaining several to be friends....

St Ann's 1st June 1848
My dear friend,

I feel sincerely thankful that you have not shown the least sign of taking offence at my freedom of sharpness in my last letter to you.... I cannot ascertain yet how soon I could be likely to see you and other friends in that quarter.... The scarcity of provision, which has for some time been bordering on famine, throughout the Island, renders it inconvenient for some of our friends to leave their families; and they must fish or do something else to provide for their daily support, to keep them from starvation. There has never been anything like this in Cape Breton. There are several among us who could, without distraction, sustain their own families, if the burden of others around them had not fallen so grievously upon their charity; but the general destitution has made it impossible, even for the most saving, to shut their ears & eyes from the alarming claims & craving of those around them, running continually from door to door, with the ghastly features of death staring in their very faces; and especially since the expected relief from Government, for both food & seed, has been a mere disappointment. But the Lord's hand is in this dispensation, tho' few understand, or take it to heart. But this is enough, on this grievous subject, for you cannot but hear enough of it from newspapers and other current reports.

...I don't know whether you have heard of our having received a letter lately from our dear son in Australia, along with about two dozens of Newspapers, of which himself is one of the Editors. There is so much in commendation of the soil & climate, and other circumstances, of that country, in said papers, that many people here, among our friends, would wish themselves settled near our Donald. And indeed, if myself had my selection of associates along with me, there would be nothing but the impracticableness of getting forward, thro' such a fearful distance, under so many & various points of inconvenience, to prevent my own removal to it, even in this evening of my days.

St Ann's 22nd Augt. 1848

We wish gratefully to acknowledge the seasonable service of the meal received from our friends there; for the time of my return from Pictou was the most destitute here through all the summer, before supplies were obtained from the U. States. And besides the relief of our own family, many a poor person frequented our house at that time, purposely for a meal, or a night's lodging, when they learned our having a supply of oatmeal. In real truth I never observed so much need helped about our family by any other providence as the said supply. My dear partner could not but see the Lord's hand in it, not merely for ourselves, but also for a number of others from different quarters, running 'to & fro,' for a morsel to eat, or a platefull to carry home. Altho' at the same time I have found it something tender for myself, to be the medium of conveying such a gift home from my good friends.... We have now the commencement of the new potatoes; but the blight has spread too far to promise but a very inferior crop, even to the earliest plants in the Island; and late planting appears to be a complete failure. The other crops promised quite favorably before the present uncommon rain, which has continued already for a whole week, and is not over yet, by means of which the wheat, in particular, begins to rust, and thereby considerably to suffer.

The Lord's hand is 'lifted up' in these steps of providence, tho' few consider his righteous intentions & warning.—But we enjoy great rest, at these times, in our religious concerns. All the name of ministers we have around us appears to be, as it were, buried out of sight.... Whatever may be the consequence, we have overflowing meetings. Our new meeting house which we thought would be, for some years, half empty, is found already too small: tho' it contains seats for 1200 hearers, besides stairs & passages, which are, at times, overflowed....

There is a good degree of excitement among my own friends here, in favor of South Australia; if our Donald would encourage them; as there is still a free passage agency from all parts of britain to that new & extensive country. And altho' it is very unlikely that it will ever take place, yet I cannot shake myself from many stirring thoughts on the subject.

I know, without hesitation, that it is a far more favorable country than this.... We enjoy more than ordinary rest at present, from religious open opposition, yet this calm results more from external restraint & incapacity on the part of opposers than from any change of disposition or internal principles; and therefore little to be depended upon by my family or friends, if I were once laid in the grave. In that case I would not choose this place (for) the fixed residence of any of my sincere adherents; if the Lord, in his good providence, would open for them a likely door of escape.... I cannot likewise, at times, avoid thinking that the Lord may have some particular dispensation in reserve (thro') the circumstance of my dear son's random emigration to that distant, vastly extended, & unoccupied country; which is both mild and healthy, with many other advantages.

St. Ann's C.B. 27th June 1849

You would, of course, have heard that we have of late very satisfactory accounts from our dear son in that distant quarter; who eagerly invites his friends to the same mild and fruitful country. And as we are fondly, tho slowly, preparing for a removal, I cannot leave home.... Indeed it is now a question to me whether I shall ever more see Pictou.... I have thought to enclose my son's letter; but I cannot now lay my hand on it, as it is seldom in the house; for its information is so interesting to all intending emigrants for that new Colony, that it is already in half tatters, by frequent perusal, from place to place...it will take a year yet, at least, before we can think of being prepared;.... To finish a vessel of the size of our frame, under existing circumstances, requires no little concern...all our best friends here are desirous of either accompanying or following us, if providence seconds their views; for otherwise I could never feel myself at freedom to abandon my sincere adherents; none of whom have any hesitation on the subject but how to get once clear of debts & obtain a passage. I believe no people would answer better in South Australia than our Scotch people, reared, in this country; and that there is no other quarter in the world which would agree more with their health & habits....

St Ann's 31st July 1851

Fleshly passions (are) likewise a fearful flood to carry away the vigor of the soul from the love & power of the truth; especially in our youth.... On this ground you can often observe young men of intelligence, and a good measure of religious edification, joining themselves, in matrimonial connection, with very shallow & silly wives, on the mere account of their bulk or bodies, vails or wimples; or the flash & feature of their little faces, without any other real virtue or wisdom to recommend them. And on the other hand, you may, at times, decern a bloomy & bland young woman spliced & sprained for life to a crabbed & corrupt knot of a husband, ensnared by his mere tattling & tickling, smirking & smiling habits, at the time of their wooing; tho' for their future lives together, they manifestly combine, in their intellectual dispositions, but a fire & water; or any other opposite elements. These are some of the sorry & sad results of fickle & fallen nature, by which the world is drowned against God, & real goodness & godliness. But I find by happy experience, as well as by the sure and sacred scriptures, that it is through the pure and powerful spirit of God in Jesus Christ, that we can ever be brought to hate & overcome our sinful inclinations & unruly propensities, our worldliness & pride.

...If I will be spared to cross the great seas, I shall think it my privilege & pleasure to write you a sketch of the scenes & circumstances of the country of our destination, in secular & religious concerns.... I wish to pray Heaven that the long continuation of your attachment to me, 'thro good report, and evil report' amidst all my failings & short comings, would be blessed to your own souls; and that any deficience in my doctrine, or example, might not prove a stumbling block to any of you. I hope I write these remarks in the sincerity of my heart, as in the sight of the Lord; and not from any false or feigned humility; altho' I feel too much of that sort of falsehood in my own mind. With joint & sincere remembrance from me, my family & friends around us, to you and all well wishing enquirers in your quarters—allowing you, at the same time, the full freedom of permitting the perusal of this letter to any of your acquaintance, according to your own inclination & discretion—

I am, my dear friend,
yours very affectionately,
N. McLeod.

"Letters of Rev. Norman McLeod, 1835-51" were published as a Bulletin *of the Public Archives of Nova Scotia, edited with an introduction by D. C. Harvey, in 1939.*

James B. Lamb

Born in 1919 in Toronto, James Lamb graduated as a naval officer from Royal Military College, Kingston, and joined the Royal Canadian Navy in 1939. During the Second World War he served aboard *HMCS Trail* and commanded the minesweeper *HMCS Minas* and corvette *HMCS Camrose*, and was mentioned in dispatches for D-Day service at Omaha Beach.

He started his writing career as a reporter and feature writer on newspapers in Woodstock, Ontario and Moose Jaw, Saskatchewan. For twenty years he was the editor and publisher of the Orillia, Ontario *Daily Packet and Times*. His 1964 editorial, "The Canada I Love: An Unfashionable Testament," is the most famous Canadian newspaper editorial of the twentieth century.

He retired to Big Harbour, Cape Breton Island in 1971 where he sailed, traveled, and wrote fifteen books, including *The Corvette Navy*, *On the Triangle Run*, and *The Other Canada*.

James Lamb died in Delta, British Columbia on February 20, 2000.